Vanishing Magic

Also by Elisabeth Beresford

Dangerous Magic
Invisible Magic

Elisabeth Beresford

Vanishing Magic

Illustrated by Ann Tout

DRAGON
GRANADA PUBLISHING
London Toronto Sydney New York

Published by Granada Publishing Limited
in Dragon Books 1979

ISBN 0 583 30269 6

First published in Great Britain by
Rupert Hart-Davis Ltd 1970

Granada Publishing Limited
Frogmore, St. Albans, Herts AL2 2NF
and
3 Upper James Street, London W1R 4BP
1221 Avenue of the Americas, New York, NY10020, USA
117 York Street, Sydney, NSW 2000, Australia
100 Skyway Avenue, Toronto, Canada M9W 3A6
110 Northpark Centre, 2193 Johannesburg, South Africa
CML Centre, Queen & Wyndham, Auckland 1, New Zealand

Made and printed in Great Britain by
Cox & Wyman Ltd, London, Reading and Fakenham
Set in Baskerville

To
Conn Ryan

Contents

1. *The Start of the Trouble*

EDWARD HOBSON had never been much good at running, as he had a bad habit of tripping over his own feet, but he ran this morning all right. As soon as the school gates were opened he was off down the street with his satchel banging against his knees and his cap falling over one eye.

'Go it, Old Four-Eyes!' somebody shouted after him, but Edward hardly heard them.

It was the start of the holidays and he was free for six wonderful weeks. Not that Edward didn't like school, he did. It was the other boys he wasn't so keen about. He couldn't help it if he was good at lessons but rotten at games—and that he would keep falling over things. And it was hardly his fault, surely, if somehow he managed to get ink all over himself, even on his ears, or if his shoelaces would keep coming undone so that the teachers too shouted at him quite a bit? And as for having bad eyes so that he had to wear spectacles—which somehow managed to get broken regularly—well that could happen to anyone. But he simply hated being called Old Four-Eyes or, what was even worse, Old Slobber-Chops. But now he was free of all that for a while and it was a lovely morning, so Edward ran through the back streets until he got a stitch and had to slow down.

He stopped at the traffic lights and watched a train go through the cutting making a swishing sound instead of the old clickety-click, because it was all continuous rail now which made the trains much smoother to ride on but somehow less exciting. The traffic stopped unwillingly as the lights changed again and Edward crossed the road and stepped onto the Common. It was rather a nice Common with trees and bushes and a big dip at one side, which Edward's grandfather could remember as a pond where he used to sail boats sixty years ago. But now it only had grass at the bottom and, if there was ever any snow, Edward used to borrow the turkey tin and go tobogganing down the banks.

Edward's grandfather had also told him that long, long ago, even before *he* was born, there were highwaymen on the road through the Common so that nobody used it after dark. But that seemed quite impossible now because the road was always busy, even in the middle of the night.

There weren't many people about and Edward stopped to watch a puppy turning somersaults and a fat pigeon trying to bully a sparrow away from some bread. And then he noticed that every fifty yards or so round the edge of the grass small wooden boards had been hammered into the ground, so he went over to have a look at one of them. A paper had been pinned onto it, but somebody had already torn off a few strips and scribbled over it, so all Edward could make out was:

NOTICE IS BY GIVEN THAT TO ROAD IDENING SCHE ART OF THE COMMON LAND ILL BE REDUCED BY ACRES. THEREFORE AS COMPENSAT AND WILL BE GIVEN BACK BY THE EMOLITION OF OUSES.

Edward tried to fill in the gaps and he was rather enjoying it when a voice behind him said.

'Hallo! I know who you are.'

The voice belonged to a small girl who was wearing a dress that was far too big for her, so she had hitched it up round the waist with a red ribbon. She had no shoes on and she had a daisy behind one ear. With her was a baby in a pram which also held some shopping, a pair of sandals and half a bottle of fizzy lemonade.

'I don't know who you are,' said Edward, rubbing a finger across his spectacles which, as usual, were rather dirty.

'Yes, you do,' the girl contradicted him, 'we're the new people in Number Five next door to you. I'm Meg, and this is Tommy, and your name's Edward, and you live with your grandfather who's an Admirable.'

'Admiral. And he's not,' contradicted Edward in his turn. 'He was the Captain of a tug-boat but now he likes to be called a Commander – and how do you know so much anyway?'

'The people told me in the shops,' said Meg. 'At least they didn't tell *me*, because people don't bother telling children things unless it's to say don't do something or hurry up. But I heard them talking. See?'

'I think so,' said Edward who had got rather lost in the middle of all this. He wasn't sure if he liked the girl or not yet. She seemed a bit inquisitive.

'I do like your house,' she said, 'it's the tidiest house I've ever seen. Would you like some fizzy lemon?'

She produced a cup without a handle from among the packets and tins and poured him out a drink. It was deliciously cold and made his nose tingle, so Edward decided that what with one thing and another she wasn't so bad after all until she said:

'Why've you got green wool round the sides of your glasses?'

'Because the side's broken so I had to make a splint for it,' Edward replied, waiting for her to start calling him Old Four Eyes.

'How clever of you,' said Meg. 'Are you good at mending things?'

'No, I'm much better at breaking 'em,' Edward replied with a deep sigh. 'Yesterday in school I just happened to trip over a book and...'

He stopped suddenly as Meg pinched his arm and pointed to the far side of the Common where some of the houses had been knocked down to make way for the new road which was being built. As it was now twelve o'clock the workmen had gone off to have their dinners and there was only one person on the site.

'See her?' whispered Meg.

'Yes, that's Miss Witcham from Number One,' said Edward, screwing up his eyes.

'Witcham,' said Meg, her own eyes now as round as marbles, 'there, I knew it. She's a witch.'

'A what?' said Edward, who didn't think he'd heard her properly.

'A witch,' repeated Meg. 'She is you know,' and she nodded her head wisely.

'Don't be silly. That's just her name. She's all right and so's her sister.'

'Well I think she is, I think they both are. And anyway what's she doing now?' demanded Meg. She was rather a lonely little girl for both her mother and father went out to work, so she often made up stories to make things more interesting when she had nobody but Tommy for company.

'How should I know?' said Edward rather crossly.

'Well go on, go and have a look,' suggested Meg, who was starting to enjoy this game.

'I can't.'

'You're afraid!'

That, of course, was too much. Edward handed back the cup and picked up his satchel, and set off across the Common with Meg and the baby following him at a safe distance. As Edward drew nearer to the houses he thought they looked rather sad, with some of their walls missing so that you could see the wallpaper in the rooms and faded patches where pictures and mirrors had once been hung. The gardens were all very overgrown, although a few plants were still pushing their faces hopefully through the trailing bushes and round the planks and broken bricks. And in the middle of all this stood the tall grey figure of Miss Witcham, with her coat caught by a bramble and her hat pushed so far over her eyes that she didn't see Edward until he reached what had once been the garden wall.

'Hallo,' said Edward, feeling rather silly.

'Who? Who?' said Miss Witcham, straightening up so suddenly that she became more entangled than ever. She pushed back her hat and snatched up her shopping basket and covered up whatever was inside it.

'It's me,' said Edward, 'from Number Six.'

He would rather have liked to ask what she was doing, because she certainly seemed to be behaving rather strangely and was now trying to hide the basket behind her. But children can't ask grown-ups they don't know very well things like that, so Edward only went on looking at her.

'Oh yes,' said Miss Witcham, 'so it is. It's Edward from the end of the Row. Dear me. For a moment I thought it was...' And she stopped.

'Who?' asked Meg from her safe position behind Edward.

'Oh them,' said Miss Witcham, waving her hand towards the building site with its row of neat new huts. 'Now if you'll excuse me I must run along. Otherwise,' and she stopped again in her odd way and began to pull herself free from the bushes but, even though this took quite a lot of doing, Meg's sharp eyes noticed that Miss Witcham somehow managed to keep her shopping basket covered.

'Careful,' said Edward as Miss Witcham tripped over a broken plank. However, she kept her balance and a moment later was hurrying off down the street at a surprising rate for such an elderly person.

'There,' said Meg triumphantly, 'she was Up To Something.'

'No she wasn't,' contradicted Edward who had known Miss Witcham and her sister nearly all his life and who suddenly felt he should stick up for them in front of a newcomer. 'I'm off to have my dinner. Thanks for the drink.'

Meg watched him go and sighed deeply. She had been hoping that she had at last found a friend, but apparently it was not to be. So she got out the lemonade and divided it very fairly in half, and gave Tommy his share out of the cup and drank her own out of the bottle. And then very slowly, because there was nothing to hurry for, she set off after Edward and Miss Witcham towards Farthing Row.

Farthing, as most people call it, is one of those odd little rows of houses which you can still find tucked away in parts of London. A hundred and fifty years ago, before the railways started, the Common had been surrounded by fields and meadows and orchards and the only house had been a beautiful Georgian Manor House owned by Lord Farthing. He was a rich man and, as he grew even richer, he had built for six of his servants six small houses actually on the Common itself. Number One was the largest, then came four little ones and then at the far end Number Six which was a little bigger than Two, Three, Four and Five but not as large as One. They all had grass and trees in front of them and long gardens at the back ending in stables and barns. And very pretty they must have looked too.

But then the railways started pushing their way out of the middle of London, and when the last Lord Farthing died his land was sold and his Manor pulled down. Slowly roads and streets began to follow the course of the railway lines, and the fields and meadows and even the orchards were swallowed up by rows and rows and rows of houses. Until finally nothing was left of the great estate except Farthing Row and that was now old and shabby and the stables and barns were often used by people for dumping their rubbish, so that instead of housing horses and carriages and tackle, they held old gas cookers and bursting mattresses and broken television sets.

The smartest house in the Row belonged to Edward's grandfather. It was painted white and blue, the hedge was trimmed and at the back there was a grass lawn with a ship's figurehead planted in the middle of it. And beyond that was the kitchen garden and one old, old apple tree which had been left over from the orchard days. There was a very high wall all along the garden side and on top of this was some wire netting. This was to try and keep out the teenage boys who played around on the Common. When they got bored with kicking a football about they often set about climbing into the garden of Number Six to pick the apples, or try to push over the figurehead, or just to trample down everything they could.

The moment Edward's grandfather saw them he would sound the alarm bell on the half-landing. This was the signal for Edward to stop whatever he was doing and to rush out into the garden with his grandfather and Jellicoe their old dog. Usually the boys would go scrambling back over the wall, breaking and bending the netting and leaving a trail of damage behind them. But once or twice recently they hadn't bothered to run, but had walked quite slowly shouting rude things and laughing at poor old Jellicoe, who was pretending to be a fierce watchdog in spite of his age.

'Well, well,' said Edward's grandfather, the Commander. 'Broken up have you? Good, good. Dinner will be on the table in three minutes exactly. Go and wash your hands, brush your hair and do up your shoelaces. Quick, smart.'

The Commander was the same height as Edward, but his clothes were always neatly pressed, even his gardening overall, and his small white beard was as smooth and silky as his white hair. There was sixty years difference in their ages and their characters were entirely different, yet they got on very well together and, as Edward couldn't remember his parents who had died in an accident when he was a baby, he was extremely happy at No. Six Farthing Row.

'Any boarders yet?' asked Edward over lunch. They called the boys off the Common 'boarders' because the Commander always treated his home like a ship. The alarm bell was the call to 'Repel boarders!'

'Not yet. No. Wait till the holidays start properly, though, and they'll be back. Won't they Jellicoe, heh?'

Jellicoe raised his shaggy grey head and growled hoarsely.

'We're going to be attacked from the other side too if we don't watch out,' went on the Commander, giving Edward another helping of apple crumble. 'Saw a girl watching me over the wall this morning. She said Hello or some such thing, but I didn't reply. Don't know her. What are you staring at, boy?'

'That,' said Edward, screwing up his eyes and looking at a small white notice which was propped up on the mantelpiece. Some of the words seemed vaguely familiar, 'Road Widening Scheme' and 'Demolition of Houses', and then he remembered suddenly and said:

'That's written up all round the Common too.'

'It's nothing to do with you. Nothing for you to worry your head about,' snapped his grandfather. 'More apple?'

'No thank you. Demolition means pulling things down. Is it about those houses on the side of the Common?'

'In a way. Stack the plates, boy. Carefully now, we don't want any more chips than we've already got. You can help me with the netting when we've done the washing-up. We must prepare for an attack. What I should really like would be a good strong naval cannon. That'd send them packing.'

'People aren't allowed guns now,' said Edward, just managing to avoid stepping on Jellicoe's tail.

'Can't do this, can't do that,' muttered his grandfather. 'Can't even stay in our own homes half the time.'

Edward was just about to ask him what he meant when he stood on one of his own shoelaces. The result was both extremely noisy and painful, although the china suffered more than Edward and, by the time everything was cleared up, he had forgotten his grandfather's words. Yet somehow, although he thoroughly enjoyed putting up the netting, Edward kept on feeling as if everything wasn't quite as it should be. It was that strange, jumpy, half-frightened feeling you get just before a thunderstorm and Edward still had it when he took Jellicoe for his evening walk across the Common.

The traffic thundered and rumbled down the road and Jellicoe went sniffing after imaginary rabbits, with Edward limping behind him because his knee still hurt. It was twilight and getting darker every minute, and it was just as they reached the big, shadowy chestnut trees that Jellicoe put back his ears and growled and Edward heard a voice say:

'Oh dear! Oh dear, oh dear! Bother it!'

And for the second time that day Edward found Miss Witcham in the abandoned garden, only now she was really trapped, for one of the planks had fallen across a bush and the bush in its turn had a firm grip on Miss Witcham.

'I'll help,' said Edward, and he scrambled over the broken wall and began to try to set her free. It was rather a painful business for no sooner had the brambles let her go than they had fastened on to Edward, and

Jellicoe, sniffing and whining round his feet, didn't make it any easier.

'Thank you *so* much,' said Miss Witcham, 'I don't know how I would have.'

'That's all right,' replied Edward and stepped backwards just as Jellicoe moved forwards, and the next moment Edward, his arms going like windmills, fell with a tremendous thud into quite a large hole. His spectacles went flying and when he at last managed to climb upright, he saw to his horror that this time they were really broken as the glass was cracked right across. It was a disaster for not only did new ones cost money it also meant that until he got them the world would be a misty unreal place to him.

'It was all my fault,' said Miss Witcham. 'All my— Only one thing to do. Come on.'

'But—' said Edward.

'No time to,' said Miss Witcham, and she seized his hand in hers and began to pull the still protesting Edward across the Common and towards her own home at No. One Farthing.

2. *Notice to Quit*

ALTHOUGH Edward had known Miss Witcham and her sister by sight for almost as long as he could remember anything, he had never been inside their home before, and he felt just a bit nervous as Miss Witcham opened the front door. After all—suppose Meg was right and they *were* witches? Two things made him decide to follow her into the house without hanging back. The first was that he was so upset about his broken spectacles he would have accepted any offer of help, and the second was Jellicoe, who didn't wait to be asked inside, but pushed his way in quite rudely with his tail waving like a flag and his tongue hanging out. And Jellicoe was a dog who usually took his time over deciding whether he liked people and places.

'Lily,' called Miss Witcham, 'it's me, Rose, and I've brought poor Edward Hobson with me, because—'

'Because I've broken my spectacles,' said Edward, who was rapidly getting used to the way in which Miss Witcham talked. He stumbled after her into the front room and then, although he only had one fairly good eye as the other felt it was looking through tissue paper because of the shattered lens, he stopped and stared.

It was like no other room he had ever seen in his life. It was crammed full of furniture and books and pictures and vases and ornaments. And they were not the usual kind of furnishings, either. Edward's one astonished eye saw among other things an enormous wooden chest covered in straps and buckles, a large, beautifully polished model of an old steam engine, a baby's wooden cot on rockers, a big red kite whose tail was draped over a rocking horse, and a stuffed fox who appeared to be stalking a white kitten which was sitting on the mantelpiece cleaning its ears.

It was the kind of room to explore and examine for hours on end, like a toyshop that is full of really interesting toys: and Edward stood in the doorway with his mouth opening and shutting while Jellicoe, luckily taking no notice of the kitten which now had its back up, picked his way through the tables and chairs and went and put his shaggy head on the lap of Miss Lily who was knitting in a chair by the fireplace.

'Good evening, Jellicoe,' said Miss Lily.

She was older and smaller than her sister, but she had the same white hair and very bright grey eyes and arched nose.

'Be back in a moment,' said Miss Rose. 'I'll just put the basket in the kitchen. I've found some most interesting.' And she was gone leaving Edward in the doorway.

'Well, Edward,' said Miss Lily, 'it's very nice to see you close to. I've often watched you through the window. Dear me, your spectacles *are* in a bad way. May I see them?'

Edward crossed the room extremely carefully and managed not to fall over anything. Miss Lily put down her knitting and took the spectacles in her bent fingers and clicked her tongue.

'I know,' Edward said gloomily, forgetting all the excitements of the strange room as he remembered the reason for his visit. 'They're really bust, aren't they?'

'Really bust,' agreed Miss Lily sadly, 'and not very safe to wear either, I'm afraid.'

'Grandfather's going to be pretty cross,' Edward said, sighing. 'The last time it happened I was playing conkers. It wasn't really my fault, but you know what conkers are.'

'Indeed I do. Fly off the string without so much as a word of warning. Was it a good conker?'

'Best one I ever had. It beat thirty-eight others. It was as hard as *iron.*'

'No wonder it broke your glasses,' said Miss Lily, stroking Jellicoe under his grey chin in a way that made him shudder with delight.

'The trouble is,' said Edward, who was becoming gloomier every second, 'that new lenses cost such a lot and...' He stopped short, rather like Miss Rose always did, as he remembered how often his grandfather had told him not to go round talking about money, or rather the lack of it. Miss Lily, however, seemed to understand perfectly.

'Everything costs a lot,' she said, nodding.

'And that's why,' said Miss Rose, suddenly appearing in the doorway, 'we've got to do something to help Edward. If he hadn't been kind enough to rescue me he wouldn't have fallen over and broken the things. It was all my fault only I did so want to get those snapdragons out of that deserted garden. I do love digging round in old gardens, they're always so full of.'

Miss Lily and Edward waited politely to see if she had finished and as Miss Rose appeared to have come to a fullstop, her elder sister said thoughtfully:

'Help, Edward? How, I wonder?'

'Couldn't you mend?' asked Miss Rose.

Miss Lily shook her head slowly.

'I don't think it would be a *wise* thing to do,' she said. 'Remember what happened that time when the gas-meter wouldn't work properly and I mended, or at least tried to mend it? When the gas-man finally did arrive he was quite upset.'

'He was astonished,' agreed Miss Rose. 'It's because they use all this modern stuff like wiring and plastic and nylon, not to mention poly-this and poly-that. It upsets.'

'Upsets what?' Edward couldn't help asking. His respect for Miss Lily was growing rapidly as he had once tried to mend his own bedside lamp and the result had been a bright blue flash, a nasty burn on his fingers, and complete darkness throughout the house. So, if an old lady like Miss Witcham could actually get a gas-meter to work, it was most remarkable.

'Upsets things,' Miss Rose said vaguely. 'I suppose your spectacles are made of poly-something?'

'They're plastic,' Edward replied, 'at least the frames

are. I know, because if you put them near something hot you can bend them. Oh well, it can't be helped, and I'd better get home if you don't mind.'

'But it *shall* be helped,' contradicted Miss Rose, looking quitè fierce. 'Lily, it's absolutely ridiculous if we cannot repay one kindness with another. If it hadn't been for Edward I might have been trapped in that garden all night; you know how unpleasant briars can be once they get old and crabby. Please Lily?'

Miss Lily hesitated, looking from her sister to Edward and then at Jellicoe, and lastly at the white kitten who was now chasing an invisible mouse.

'Well,' she said, 'I suppose—but goodness knows where it will end. Meddling with modern equipment so often leads to trouble and difficulties, as you well know, Rose. In the old days one knew where one was with wood and silver and even gold, but it's all so different now. I suppose Edward is to be trusted?'

'Trusted! What an idea! Of course he is.' Miss Rose threw up her hands in horror and Edward, feeling rather hurt, echoed her words.

'Course you can trust me.'

Miss Lily grew rather pink and jabbed at her ball of wool with the big needles and rolled up her knitting.

'Oh very well,' she said, 'only don't blame me, that's all. I shall have to borrow the spectacles, just for tonight. Edward, don't look so worried. You can have them back first thing in the morning, good as new.'

'Good as new,' agreed Miss Rose, nodding violently.

It was two against one, and although Edward felt a little doubtful about Miss Rose being able to mend his glasses after what he had just heard, any offer of help was better than none. So he said thank you very much and took the reluctant Jellicoe off by the scruff of his neck. Luckily for him his grandfather was watching a programme on television about the Royal Navy and enjoying it very much in his own way.

'Nonsense, absolute nonsense,' he said to the flickering screen. 'Never seen such nonsense in all my life. That young feller doesn't know what he's talking about. You're late, Edward. Off you go to your bunk. Jellicoe lie down, sir. Don't forget to wash your neck and clean your teeth, boy, and breakfast will be at eight sharp. Can't have any slacking even if you are on leave. Absurd, complete rubbish, I've a good mind to write to the television people and complain.'

Edward had a somewhat painful bath owing to the scratches on his legs. He lay in bed listening to the crackling sound of the television set in the room below and the steady rumble of traffic on the main road which crossed the Common. He heard the distant 'dee-da dee-da dee-da' of a police car siren, and a jet airliner thundering overhead as it made for London airport, and a motor cyclist going much too fast round the corner of Farthing Lane. And then, just for a moment, it was as though all these familiar night noises had been switched off and instead Edward heard, or thought he heard, someone singing very softly. It was a very pleasant tune and Edward sat up in bed and stared at the shifting patterns which the trees were making on his window. And then the singing stopped and all the old sounds came back again.

'Funny,' thought Edward, 'must've been the radio from next door I suppose.'

By a quarter to eight Edward was standing on the doorstep of Number One with his fingers crossed for luck. Miss Rose Witcham opened the door with a kettle in one hand and the white kitten under her other arm.

'You *are* an early,' she said.

'I had to come before breakfast,' Edward explained.

'Grandfather didn't notice last night because he was busy, but he'd be bound to notice now that I hadn't got my spectacles on. Are they – ?'

'Done? Well my sister thinks so,' said Miss Rose cautiously. 'Come in and see for yourself.'

Miss Lily was wearing a faded pink dressing-gown and a hair-net and she looked a little tired, but Edward didn't see this because without his spectacles everything was blurred.

'Done,' said Miss Lily, 'and what a job they were too. Would you like to try them on, Edward?' and she handed him his spectacles. She had made a very good job of them. Not only was the glass all in one piece again but the knitting wool had gone from the side.

'Gosh,' said Edward, 'I say!'

'Don't say *anything* until you've put them on,' said Miss Lily. 'I can't help feeling just a little anxious, because it's such a long time since I tried anything quite like this and I'm not at all sure that I've done it correctly. Glass can be tricky.'

'But how did you do it?' asked Edward. Up till this very minute he hadn't really believed that Miss Lily could possibly mend his spectacles properly. The most he had hoped for was that she might be able to make the cracks look a bit better. But there were no signs of cracks at all. The lenses were all in one piece and the specs had a kind of sparkle about them. As they were usually rather dirty and misty this was remarkable enough in itself.

'Ask no questions and you'll be told no,' said Miss Rose from the doorway. 'Drat, the kettle's boiling over. Excuse.'

She put down the kitten which promptly curled up and went to sleep under the rocking-horse looking exactly like a ball of white furry wool.

'Go on,' urged Miss Lily and Edward picked up the spectacles and put them on his nose and, as he did so, he felt a very slight tingle. He didn't notice this at once because suddenly the soft, blurred world came back into focus and after twelve hours he could see properly again.

'Well?' asked Miss Lily, jabbing at him with one of her bent fingers.

'Gosh,' said Edward again. It was most odd, but somehow he felt as if he was seeing everything much more clearly than he had ever done before. He saw Miss Lily and the pink dressing-gown and net, and all the furniture, but the strange thing was that the chest and the rocking-horse and quite a few other things were shadowy as though he were looking through them. Edward shut his left eye, but it didn't make any difference so he opened it again and shut his right eye.

'Well?' asked Miss Lily anxiously.

'They're smashing,' said Edward. 'I mean, they're as good as new—only better somehow.'

'In what way better?' asked Miss Lily, quite sharply for her.

'They're so clean,' Edward replied. 'It makes everything look, well, sharp.'

'Told you,' said Miss Rose, bobbing back into the doorway and beaming at her sister. 'You always were the clever one, Lily. I knew you could do it.'

A bell clanged in the distance and Edward stopped puzzling over the strange mistiness of the furniture and jumped to attention.

'Breakfast, and I promised I wouldn't be late. Thanks most awfully, Miss Witcham. Thank you very much indeed. Thank you.'

'Well,' said Miss Rose as the front door banged behind Edward, 'there you see. Everything's as right as.'

Miss Lily shifted uncomfortably in her chair and rubbed her bent fingers together.

'I'm not sure,' she said. 'He looked odd, Rose, when he put them on. He's not the usual sort of boy. Supposing something goes wrong?'

'Nothing will. Come and have your breakfast, Lily, and stop worrying, do. You're just overtired and I don't wonder at it, up half the night working. What you need is a good rest. I don't suppose we shall hear any more about.'

Miss Rose might have been a little less sure of herself if she could have seen Edward at that moment. He had just started on his cornflakes and the spoon was halfway to his mouth when he noticed the piece of paper on the mantelpiece. It had slid out from its hiding place behind the clock and Edward found to his surprise that, although he was sitting several feet away from it on the other side of the room, he could read all the print quite clearly.

'Crumbs!' said Edward.

'Don't talk with your mouth full,' said Commander Hobson.

'I'm not. I haven't started eating yet.'

'Then get on with it, boy.'

Edward took a spoonful of cereal, his eyes still fixed on the paper and all his relief over the mending of the spectacles vanished as he read the words.

'Demolition order. In order to repay the Common land which has been taken away by the building of the new road extension, Numbers one to six Farthing Row are to be demolished. This order will take effect from...' The rest of the words were hidden by a model of HMS *Victorious*, but Edward had read enough to take in what the notice was all about. His house and all the others in the row were going to be pulled down. It was as though a cold hand had suddenly settled on Edward's shoulder and he felt a shiver go right down his back.

Unless something could be done to save it Farthing Row was doomed and they would all be homeless.

3. *Edward Vanishes*

'I DON'T believe it,' said Meg.

'It's true all right,' said Edward, 'the notice was printed, so it *must* be true. Besides it's written up all round the edge of the Common on posters.'

'But we've only just come to live here,' objected Meg,

'and anyway you can't just turn people out of their homes. I bet it's against the law.'

Edward turned this idea over in his mind and shook his head.

'There's probably another law that says they can.'

Meg scowled horribly at the shabby pram where Tommy was trying to clap his hands and eat a biscuit at the same time. Most of the biscuit was going over his clothes and Meg sighed and knelt up and tried to clean him with a paper handkerchief.

'I asked Grandfather about it,' Edward went on, kicking at the grass with one heel and making a muddy patch, 'and he got quite cross and said it was nothing to do with me, but it jolly well is because I like living here and I like the Common and I don't want to leave it, ever.'

'It's not bad,' Meg agreed, taking away the remains of the biscuit and finishing it herself. 'I wish we could do something to stop it happening. Tommy, stop that you bad boy, you can't eat carrots till they've been cooked. Put it down.'

Tommy got rid of the carrot by throwing it out of the pram and at the same time Edward said:

'Yes, I wish we jolly well could find a way!'

At that exact moment he and Meg were sitting on the grass by the end of the garden wall of Number Six. It was a fairly safe place to sit as it had some rather tired-looking bushes growing up against it, while further along, where there were no bushes, some teenage boys had chalked up two football posts on the brickwork and were trying to kick a ball between them. Edward was very carefully not looking at the footballers because earlier on he had recognized some of them as the boys who climbed over the wall and who often shouted rude things at him. So instead he was staring rather absentmindedly at the familiar wall behind the bushes, and then for the second time that morning he had the strange feeling that he could see straight through it.

Edward gently took off his spectacles and screwed up his eyes and at once the wall became rather blurred, but definitely not misty. So he put his specs on again and got to his feet and went over to investigate. The nearer he came to the wall the more certain he grew that everything was not as it should be for, in spite of the strong sunlight, there was a deep grey patch on the bricks that he had never noticed before.

'Dry rot,' said Edward who had heard his grandfather use those words about part of the wall under the kitchen sink. That particular patch had smelt unpleasant and had been pulled down by the local builder who had put in new bricks and then sent the Commander a bill that had made him give up smoking his pipe for three very short-tempered months.

'I do hope it isn't,' said Edward, remembering all this and he put out his hand to touch the misty grey patch. The next second he had jumped at least two feet backwards as for one dreadful moment his hand had quite literally vanished. His arm and even his wrist had been perfectly normal, but his hand just had not been there at all. Edward looked at it now and wriggled his fingers about and then bit one. The bite was real enough, in fact, in his anxiety, he had been a little too thorough.

'Ouch,' he exclaimed.

'What *are* you doing?' asked Meg, dusting the carrot on her skirt. 'Jumping about and biting yourself. Have you been stung?'

'No, well, that is,' said Edward, 'it's that patch there. Look!'

'I can't see anything,' replied Meg, coming over. 'Is this a new game?'

'That patch there,' said Edward, who was rapidly getting over his fright at having had an invisible hand, 'where it's all misty, can't you see?'

'Oh yes,' said Meg, 'course I can. That bit with a rainbow in it I suppose.'

Her voice had exactly the same note in it that Edward had heard a hundred times before in the voices of the boys at school, and the last of his fright disappeared in temper as he shouted:

'Well, just you jolly well watch,' and he rushed at the wall with both hands stretched out in front of him, completely forgetting to look where his feet were going, so they tripped over the bottom of the bush and before Edward could stop himself he went headlong into the wall. Or, in fact, right through it. One moment he was there and the next there was nothing to see but the bush settling back into position and behind it the apparently solid brickwork.

'Edward?' said Meg in a very small voice. 'Edward?'

'Ed, Ed, Ed, Ed,' agreed Tommy, picking up a tin of peas and trying to chew it.

'Don't,' said Meg. She had gone very pale and her knees were trembling, so she held on to the pram and took away the tin without taking her eyes off the wall.

'It was a very clever trick,' she said. 'I don't know how you did it, Edward, but please come back. Please come back NOW.'

The bush stopped shaking and the football thudded against the wall further along and two of the boys started fighting over it, but there was no sign of Edward and Meg slowly sat down on the grass with her feet straight out in front of her and her mouth open.

Meanwhile Edward was behaving in very much the same way. He was quite sure that he had either gone completely mad, or that he was dreaming, for the place in which he found himself was exactly like a dream. He was surrounded by little trails of mist that were in all the colours of the rainbow. Like puffs of smoke caught in a slight breeze they formed themselves into little clouds, grew bigger and then thinner until they were hardly there at all and then re-formed again. A pink cloud floated past him and Edward put out his hand to touch it and found that it was surprisingly firm, rather like foam rubber. He let it go again and it drifted away and grew larger and melted into a pale yellow cloud that slowly turned into orange.

'How, how, how?' asked Edward and was further startled by the sound of his own voice. He shut his eyes as tightly as he could and counted up to ten and then opened them again. A long, wispy green cloud floated under his feet and gently bounced him up and down.

'This is impossible,' said Edward huskily, 'and I don't believe it. I just don't.'

It was one thing to discover a patch of dry rot on a garden wall and quite another to find yourself suddenly surrounded by coloured clouds and Edward, being an intelligent boy, knew for certain that nobody, not even an astronaut, can actually stand on clouds. So the situation in which he found himself was quite impossible, the only trouble being that it was actually happening.

'Please,' said Edward, trying to speak calmly, 'I'd like to go back now.'

Nothing happened except that a small violet cloud turned itself into a misty purple and sank slowly into a long trail of scarlet. The result was extremely lovely but no help at all. Edward tried pinching himself and that was no use either, except that it was quite painful, so he stamped and the green cloud obligingly bounced him upwards. Edward staggered slightly and then stood stiff as a ramrod and, with his hands clenched by his sides, said very loudly indeed:

'Oh I wish I was back on the common, I wish I'd never...'

'Edward,' Meg shrieked, 'you're horrible, I hate you, that was a horrid trick!'

She was scrambling to her feet right in front of him and, like a lot of people when they've had a bad fright, she was in a dreadful temper. There was not a cloud in sight, except the ordinary white ones dotted about in the blue sky and one of the footballers yelled at Meg.

'That's right, have a go at him. Silly Old Four Eyes.'

'Silly Old Four Eyes, silly Old Four Eyes,' chanted some of the other boys.

Edward stared at them and then at the very solid green ground under his feet and then at Meg and lastly at Tommy who had gone to sleep sucking the corner of a detergent packet.

'Where've I been?' Edward whispered.

'I don't know and I don't want to,' Meg said crossly. 'I suppose it was a very clever thing to do, but don't do it again.'

'Do what?'

'Go through the wall. *You* know, *you* did it.'

And Meg began to push the pram across the Common, still too upset to notice what Tommy was doing, which wasn't a bit like her.

'Now look here,' said Edward, catching up with her, 'I honestly don't know what happened and it wasn't a trick. At least it wasn't a trick that I did. Somebody else must have.'

'Me, I suppose! Or Tommy!'

'I don't know. The wall just seemed to go all misty and I went through and there was nothing but clouds. Coloured clouds. I was standing on one. It was green.'

Meg stopped pushing and looked at him scornfully.

'Pull the other leg,' she said, 'you've been seeing things.'

'Well I jolly well did see,' said Edward and stopped and put his hand up to his spectacles, as he suddenly remembered how when he had taken them off the misty patch had vanished. 'My specs,' Edward shouted, 'that's IT.'

'What is? Don't shout, people are looking at us.'

'It's my specs,' Edward said in a hurried whisper. 'I broke them last night and Miss Witcham mended them for me and she told me she wasn't sure if she'd done them right. And she hasn't. When I've got them on I can see things that other people can't. Here, you try.' And he took them off and held them out to Meg who backed away quickly.

'Not likely,' she said, 'they might be dangerous. And anyway I don't believe...'

'It was you who thought they were witches,' interrupted Edward growing more and more excited, 'and they are, at least sort of. I'm going to tell them what's happened. You needn't come.'

At which Meg instantly decided that nothing would keep her away. She still didn't believe a quarter of what Edward had told her, but it wasn't nearly dinner-time yet and now that it was no longer frightening this was an unusual and interesting game.

'All right I will,' said Meg, 'I can pretend things just as good as you. Tommy, stop sucking that. It's for washing your clothes, not your insides.'

Miss Rose Witcham was working in the front garden, putting in the plants which she had collected the evening before. She took one look at Edward's face and said:

'Oh dear! What has?'

'Can't tell you out here,' said Edward. 'This is Meg and Tommy.'

'You'd better come inside then. I knew there was something not quite, but I didn't like to mention it because. My sister's having a little nap so if you could be rather quiet...'

Miss Rose led them into the kitchen at the back of the house and Meg had some difficulty in getting the pram down the narrow passage but, as she didn't want Tommy suddenly vanishing too, she was determined to take him with her. The kitchen was rather dark and shabby and there was a most unusual looking washing machine in one corner. Edward glanced at it and then stared at it. Miss Rose sat down at the scrubbed wooden table and shook her head.

'Is it?' she said.

Edward nodded.

'Misty,' he agreed.

'Never mind,' said Miss Rose, 'it works very well all the same. I thought you were an unusual boy, Edward. We both did. It's the spectacles, isn't it?'

So for the second time Edward described exactly what had happened to him and Miss Rose listened carefully until he had reached the end of his story.

'Fancy,' she exclaimed at the finish. 'Well I never.'

'Do you *believe* him?' Meg asked, 'about the clouds and everything?'

'Oh yes. Mind, I've never come across a case quite like this before and my sister did use—however that's neither here nor. Still no bones broken, no harm done, although I'm sorry you had such a nasty fright.'

'But I didn't,' replied Edward, who had been thinking things over. 'I was *surprised*, but I wasn't frightened exactly. I didn't feel as if anything dangerous was going to happen. It was quite fun really, but surprising.'

'It would be,' agreed Miss Rose.

'*I* was frightened,' said Meg. 'I was ever so frightened. People shouldn't just vanish like that. It's nasty.'

'Quite,' agreed Miss Rose soothingly. 'I don't mean to interfere, dear, but should your little brother be sucking that tin of sardines? It can't be good for him I feel. Not while they're still inside the tin anyway.'

'It's his teeth,' said Meg, sighing, 'he eats everything. I caught him with my hair slide yesterday. It's very trying.'

'So it must be. Now let me see if I can find.'

Miss Rose got to her feet and began opening cupboard doors and Edward, who felt that they were straying from the matter in hand, tried to bring the meeting back to order by saying:

'But supposing it happens again? I could vanish anywhere. At home or in school or on the football pitch. Not that I'd mind that because I'm not very good at it. My feet kick each other and not the ball, I don't know why. But...'

'Exactly,' said a voice from the doorway and they all turned round to see Miss Lily standing there leaning on a stick. She had taken off her pink hair-net, but she was still in her dressing-gown and her sharp grey eyes were fastened on Edward.

'I've been listening,' she said, 'and very interesting it was, too. Good morning, Meg, good morning, Tommy. I was perfectly well aware that I hadn't got all the right ingredients, but they are so difficult to come by these days and glass always was troublesome. However, that is not the point. The point is, Edward, what were you talking about just before all this vanishing business started?'

'I don't know,' Edward replied, frowning.

'I do,' said Meg. 'It was about the Row being pulled

down and I said I wished we could do something and Edward said...'

'I wished I could find a way to...' Edward began and then ended in a splutter as Miss Lily put her hand over his mouth.

'That explains it,' she said. 'Don't speak for a moment, Edward, you never know what might happen. Magic never manages to be straightforward somehow. So you know about the demolition order, do you?'

Edward nodded violently, afraid to speak, although Miss Lily had now removed her hand.

'Could they really turn us out?' Meg asked anxiously.

The two Miss Witchams sighed and looked so downcast that no answer was needed.

'Couldn't you do something?' Meg asked. 'I mean as you are—as you um. That is if you know what I mean.' She finished rather lamely as she wasn't at all sure if it was actually polite to call people witches and as, like Edward, she now felt as though she had known them all her life and found them very easy to get on with. It was almost like talking to grown-up people who remembered what it was to be a child, and who understood at once what you were trying to say without having to have it all explained.

'My dear, we *have* tried,' said Miss Rose earnestly. 'The difficulty is that we are so out of date. You have no idea the mess you can get into when you begin mixing what we were taught with modern methods. Oh the trouble we had with the Gas Board! And if that washing machine ever goes wrong, well we should be in the.'

'Soup. I see, at least I think I see,' Meg said cautiously.

'Syrup,' corrected Miss Rose, handing her a bottle of pale yellow liquid, 'for Tommy's teeth. It won't do him a scrap of harm and he will find it very soothing. Where were?'

'We,' put in Miss Lily who was frowning deeply. 'Exactly, Rose! Edward was wishing—a very dangerous habit, you know, which can land you in the most outlandish places—that he could find a way to save our homes. And what happens? The spectacles obey! They take him through the wall.'

There was a long pause while everybody thought this over and Tommy contentedly drank out of the bottle which Miss Rose had given him.

'Yes, but,' said Edward, frowning even harder than Miss Lily had done, 'I don't see how clouds in all different colours can possibly help. Do you?'

'Not exactly,' Miss Lily agreed, 'but obviously something wants to, or it wouldn't have happened at all. Of course, of course. What a silly old fool I am. It's the Common itself, Edward. Don't you see?'

'No,' said Edward stolidly.

'My dear boy, it's perfectly simple. Everything has a mind of its own however small, and the Common I daresay has a very broad mind indeed. It was doing its best to help, poor thing, but you didn't give it the right directions. Edward, you can save us all...'

'Always said he was a most unusual boy,' put in Miss Rose, nodding at Meg in a pleased manner.

'Me?' said Edward in a small voice.

'Yes, yes, yes,' Miss Lily knocked her stick against the kitchen floor impatiently. 'It was trying to tell you as plainly as it could that you could save Farthing Row. There must be some secret it holds which only you can find.'

'Who, me?' said Edward in an even smaller voice.

Three pairs of eyes looked in his direction, Tommy having already nodded off to sleep over his bottle.

Nobody had ever looked at him in quite that way before and Edward began to feel both proud and a little scared at this unexpected responsibility.

'The Common likes you,' said Miss Rose.

'It needs you,' said Miss Lily.

'Oh go on, Edward,' said Meg, 'do try, please?'

Edward drew a deep breath and then let it go.

'All right,' he said slowly, 'only if it all comes out wrong don't say I didn't warn you, that's all!'

4. *The First Journey*

It was a very comfortable feeling to know that the Common liked him and all through lunch Edward couldn't help smiling to himself every now and again. His grandfather was puzzled by this sudden change of mood. Edward had been very upset at breakfast time, but now apparently all his worry about being turned out of his home was forgotten.

'Children have short memories,' the Commander thought a little sadly. 'Still, it's just as well that the boy's not fretting. It's my responsibility to find us a new home, not his. I must decide on a course of action.'

He sighed. He was getting to be an old man and he had lived in the Row all his life and was fond of it. He didn't welcome the idea of having to start afresh in some new neighbourhood.

'Don't worry, Grandfather,' said Edward, 'it'll be all right. I know it will.'

'Worry? Who's worrying?' the Commander said shortly and he squared his shoulders. 'It won't be the first time I've had to abandon ship. Finish up your pudding, boy, I've important business to attend to.'

Half an hour later the Commander marched out of the house looking extremely smart and, as soon as his small figure was out of sight, Edward raced out of the back door and whistled softly. Jellicoe, who had been sleeping under the shade of the old apple tree, stirred and yawned and returned to his dreams as Meg's face appeared over the wall which divided the gardens of Numbers Six and Five.

'Has he gone?' she asked anxiously. She was rather afraid of Edward's grandfather. He always looked so stern. Edward nodded and Meg slithered out of sight to reappear again at the front door just as Edward opened it. She had never been inside his house before and her eyes widened in admiration as she saw how tidy it was.

'Isn't it clean?' she said. 'Our house is clean too, of course, but it's not quite like this.'

And nor was it. Meg's father didn't earn very much

as a van driver, so her mother had to go out to work too, and although she did her best there was no doubt about it that the Commander's best was a great deal better. Meg tried to help as much as she could but, with Tommy to look after and quite a bit of shopping to do, there never seemed to be much time somehow.

'Come and help me finish the brass,' said Edward, leading the way into the kitchen. This was one of his regular jobs and he quite enjoyed polishing away at the big bell and the telescope, not to mention all the bits and pieces which the Commander had collected on his travels.

'Well?' said Meg, settling down at the table and breathing heavily on a brass pot and then polishing it on her sleeve.

'Not like that,' Edward protested, 'there's proper stuff to put on it with a brush. I'll show you. Miss Rose says I'm to wait for orders. She says they've got to do some homework before we get started.'

'We?' Meg looked alarmed.

'You're going to help, aren't you? You don't want to move, do you?'

'Well, no, but,' Meg twisted her ankles round the legs of the chair. She didn't much care for the idea of getting too mixed up in magic, because she had an uneasy feeling that something might go wrong.

'Look here,' said Edward, suddenly looking alarmingly like his grandfather, 'if you don't want to do anything you'd better say so now. That's the cloth for polishing.'

'Oh I do, I do, but you're the one with the specs,' said Meg, suddenly seeing a way out of this difficult situation. 'I wonder what your orders will be. Mind *out*, Edward...'

The tin of polish was just saved from falling off the

table, although some of it did manage to get spilt and for several days after that the food in the Hobson household had a rather unusual tang to it. Something else which was unusual was that the Commander kept on having business appointments, and after each one he came home looking sterner than ever. Edward guessed that it was something to do with the house and wisely didn't ask any questions, but he began to fret with impatience to hear from Miss Witcham. She finally arrived at exactly the same moment as three boys climbed over the wall from the Common and went crashing across the garden.

'Repel boarders!' shouted Edward, racing for the bell and giving it a hearty ring. His grandfather came slowly out of the front room and instead of rushing out into the garden with a rolling-pin or a telescope, or whatever came to hand, he only said:

'It doesn't matter.'

'But they're in the garden!'

'Soon there won't be any garden to worry about, my boy,' said the Commander and went back into the room and shut the door. Edward had never been so shocked in all his life, and for a moment he just stood there; then he heard Jellicoe barking and yelping so he ran down the stairs and out to the back as Miss Witcham, closely followed by Meg, pushed open the front door which wasn't properly closed.

'Help!' cried Edward. 'We're being attacked.'

An old lady and a small girl weren't likely to frighten off three quite large boys, but Edward was desperate.

'Dear me,' said Miss Rose. 'By all means let us see what.'

The boys, who were breaking pieces off the apple tree and kicking at the snarling Jellicoe at the same time, turned and jeered.

'Silly Old Four Eyes.'

'Come on then,' said the largest boy, doubling up his fists and laughing, 'who's going to hit me first?'

'I am,' said Edward, nearly tripping down the steps in his haste.

'Stop!' ordered Miss Rose. She lifted her arm and pointed one finger straight at the boys, who halted in their tracks and became so still that they looked exactly as if they were playing statues. Miss Rose muttered something under her breath and the intruders, moving like sleep-walkers, went over to the wall, clambered up it and disappeared back on to the Common.

'Well,' said Edward.

'How *did* you do it?' asked Meg.

'It's quite easy really, once you've got the knack,' said Miss Rose, dusting her fingers together. 'It's like riding a bicycle, once you know how to you never forget although you may wobble a bit. I don't *think* I wobbled then, although I haven't used that trick in years. Now then, Edward. I've got.'

'My orders?' asked Edward, trying to soothe Jellicoe who was still trembling and panting—partly out of rage and partly because he was short of breath.

'Correct. Lily had been looking things up—the local library are so good about finding reference books, that.'

'Books about magic?' asked Edward. He was sure he'd get a very short answer if he went into the library and asked for a book on useful spells.

'No, local history. What a lovely garden, Edward. Cutting all that grass must be hard work. And we came to the conclusion that Time is probably the answer if the Common is willing to help. And you too, naturally.'

'Time?' said Edward, who liked to take things one *at* a time.

'Yes. The answer to our problem undoubtedly lies in the past. You will have to look for it.'

'In the past?' echoed Edward, feeling very stupid which was unlike him.

'You mean in history?' suggested Meg. 'Like we learn at school?'

'More or less,' agreed Miss Rose, 'although some of it I can assure you is not at all like what you are taught. The stories I could tell. However.'

'What part of the past?' asked Edward, who wasn't at all sure that he liked the whole idea.

'We decided the beginning was the best place to start,' said Miss Rose briskly. 'That is, the beginning of people using the Common. We felt nothing could be gained by investigating before that because of the wild.'

'Animals,' said Edward, swallowing as he vaguely remembered that wolves and boars had once lived in England. 'But what do I do exactly?'

'You merely ask your spectacles to take you where you wish to go. It's perfectly simple. Just give them the date and the Common will do the rest.'

'Will I have to go alone?' Edward asked in a low voice.

'Not necessarily, no. You can take a trusted companion, or two if you wish, but you will have to choose them carefully. I'd like to come myself, I haven't been on a voyage for years, but I'm not so young as I was and.'

There was a long, long silence while the three of them looked straight ahead down the sunny garden. Edward had now firmly decided in his own mind that he didn't want to start this adventure, but how could he possibly get out of it without looking a dreadful coward? Then he remembered that the Common was on his side, so to speak, and that a number of people were depending on him to save their homes, so he gave the most enormous sigh and said stolidly:

'OK. I'll do it.'

'Good boy,' said Miss Rose warmly. 'Is there anybody who?'

'No,' said Edward, 'I'd better go alone. There's nobody else I could trust you see.'

'There's me,' said Meg in a small voice, 'as long as you're sure it's safe. My mother'd be furious if I was captured by pirates or anything.'

'There weren't any pirates in the middle of London,' said Miss Rose. 'Although.'

'And could Tommy come too?' interrupted Meg. 'I couldn't leave him alone you see. I've promised to keep an eye on him.'

'I suppose so,' Miss Rose said doubtfully, 'babies always travel well, just like children. All children are timeless and can find their feet in any century. It's an asset we lose in later life, unfortunately. Well, Edward?'

'Are you sure?' Edward asked.

'Yes,' said Meg bravely. 'I'll come. Just to see what it's like. Hold on a minute and I'll go and get Tommy. We won't be gone for long will we, because it's getting on for his tea-time.'

'Take or give a second or two you shouldn't be away for more than five minutes at the outside,' replied Miss Rose.

'But we won't find anything as quickly as that,' Edward objected. 'It takes me longer to look for my school books some mornings.'

'Yes, but you won't be using any time in the present,' Miss Rose said, 'you'll be using past time. Not *now* time. On the first journey you made you probably felt you were away for quite a lengthy period, but to Meg it may have seemed quite short.'

'That's right,' Meg agreed, 'it wasn't very long. But where did Edward go then?'

'Oh dear,' Miss Rose wrinkled up her forehead, 'how can I explain. Edward didn't give any directions you see, so the Common just took him nowhere in particular. Do you?'

'I think so,' said Meg doubtfully and vanished into her own home, carefully shutting the door behind her so that Miss Witcham and Edward couldn't see that it was a bit untidy. By the time she returned with Tommy in his pram the other two had had a brief and hurried conversation.

'Not pirates of course,' Miss Rose whispered, 'but I didn't want to put her off, courage should always be encouraged, but you'll have to take care of her, Edward.'

'Where shall we do it?' Meg asked nervously as she wheeled out Tommy.

'As there's nobody about, here's as good a place as. Hold hands, yes with Tommy too, but don't wake him up because he must have his eyes shut. Shut yours, Meg. The spectacles have got to work for all three of you as it were. Now then, Edward, wish to find the way to 500 BC. It's a nice round.'

'Date,' said Edward and wished—quickly before he could lose his nerve. Meg's hand was trembling coldly in his, but Tommy's was nice and warm. The misty patch formed right before him this time, growing and quivering in the sunny front garden. Edward took a deep breath and gently pushed the others towards it, which was not easy because of the pram. He took one last look over his shoulder at Miss Witcham who was nodding and smiling and then the mist closed round him and he caught a glimpse of the swirling coloured clouds: and then they too vanished and he saw not the old familiar Common and the fronts of Farthing Row but a great many trees which grew so close together that the sunlight could hardly get through.

'We're there,' said Edward in a voice which didn't sound like his own.

'It's a f-forest,' said Meg in a trembling whisper. 'Something's gone wrong and I don't like it and I want to go home. Now.'

'Well you can't,' Edward replied sternly, 'and it must be the Common – only before it was one. Our history teacher at school said England was once nearly all trees, but I didn't believe him till now because it was so difficult to imagine. It's quite a *nice* forest really.'

'It's got a funny smell,' said Meg, sniffing. It had, too, for the forest was older than man and it had been growing and rotting and growing again for thousands of years, without being disturbed very much. The smell was like a mixture of one of the tropical glasshouses at Kew Gardens and the compost heap which Edward's grandfather kept behind the raspberry canes at Number Six, so it was almost familiar.

'We can't just stand here,' said Edward, wishing that he had asked Miss Rose for rather fuller instructions as to what they were to look *for*. 'Let's move on a bit, only we'd better keep close together.'

There was no need for him to say that as Meg had every intention of not letting Edward out of her sight for so much as a second. They were in the middle of a small clearing and as Edward looked up at the tall, dark trees, many of which were covered in creepers and had large mushroom-like things growing round their trunks, he found it quite impossible to believe that this was really where Farthing Row was.

'No – will be. No – is,' he muttered to himself, frowning. The international date line was hard enough to understand and that only dealt with twenty-four invisible hours. So trying to cross nearly two and a half thousand years was even more difficult; Edward gave up the struggle and decided there and then not to worry his head about it any more.

They moved very slowly for the ground was bumpy and they were not at all sure what they were going to find. A patch of deep blue caught Meg's eye and she went forward cautiously to investigate. She found what looked like a clump of bluebells only rather larger and more ragged than the usual kind.

'Aren't they pretty?' Meg said, quite forgetting to be scared. 'Do you think I could pick some? There aren't any flowers to pick in London except daisies.'

'I shouldn't think it'd matter,' Edward replied, feeling that the people of 500 BC probably weren't half as fussy about keeping off the grass and 'doing wilful damage'—whatever *that* was—as the people of his own time.

So Meg picked a whole armful of the flowers which had a clear, sweet smell and, when a perfectly ordinary bumble-bee came buzzing heavily round her bouquet, she flapped it away without worrying and went to show Tommy what she had got.

'Ed, Ed, Ed,' babbled Tommy who had woken up and was chewing his plastic rattle, then he burst out laughing as a large red butterfly came fluttering down to sit on the pram handle.

'He likes it here, don't you lovey?' said Meg. 'There aren't any nasty old noisy buses and motorbikes are there?'

It was astonishingly quiet, for apart from the call of the birds far up in the tree-tops and a distant thumping, there was no sound at all, and as Meg had lived in a town all her life she had never before been without the steady roar of traffic.

Edward wandered on a little further and, just as he realized that the trees had begun to thin out straight ahead of him, and was about to call to Meg, the thumping sound grew rapidly louder and the next moment Meg began to scream in a high-pitched way that made Edward feel as cold as stone.

'It's a wild animal, it's an elephant, it's going to eat us.'

Edward dodged back round the trees, his heart thundering, and then he stopped dead. On the other side of the clearing, its enormous horns covered in trailing vines, its great body heaving, he saw the monster looking directly back at him. It was standing between himself and Meg and the pram and it is to Edward's everlasting credit that it never even occurred to him to use the spectacles to get out of the fix he was in without waiting for the others. Instead, a deep frown gathered between his eyes as he hazily tried to remember a picture in his geography book.

'It's—it's an oxen. No an ox.'

'I don't care what it is, take it away,' wailed Meg.

'It won't hurt,' said Edward. 'It's sort of like a cow that's all. It doesn't eat people, only grass and things like that.'

As though in agreement the monster lowered its vast head and tried to scratch away the leaves which were tickling its face.

'There,' said Edward, as if he was talking to Jellicoe, 'you've got yourself in a right old mess, haven't you?' And he walked across the clearing and slowly put out his hand and began to unwind the creepers, while Meg watched him with her mouth wide open in admiration and surprise.

5. *Taken Prisoner*

MEG had to admit that the ox was a very gentle creature and although she had never seen a cow, except on television, it did appear to have the same placid nature in spite of its enormous size. In fact, once it was released from its garlands, it showed a distinct desire to be friends and, as the small party made its way out of the forest, Edward had to turn round more than once to order it *not* to keep treading on his heels. The ox looked at him with large, calm brown eyes, snorted softly and hung back for a moment or two and then did exactly the same thing all over again.

'I've got enough trouble with my own feet without you making it worse,' grumbled Edward.

'Oh look,' said Meg, stopping short, 'it's people. I hope they're friendly too.'

Before them was quite a large open space, most of which was roughly divided into small plots of land on which various crops were being grown in rather straggly lines. Edward, who had often helped his grandfather to lay out neat rows of vegetables with the aid of a piece of string and two sticks, decided that somebody really ought to show these people how to get a straight line. But almost at the same instant he realized that he could hardly suggest that he'd nip down to Woolworths and buy some twine because there wouldn't be any Woolworths and probably no twine either. All this went through his head in a flash, even as he noticed that in the very centre of the small fields there was a collection of round wooden huts with no windows and just a hole in the roof to let out the smoke.

The people were small and very sunburned and were mostly somewhat skimpily dressed in roughly woven clothes, although one or two of them were wearing sheepskins that had been dyed red or blue. There were also several babies and small children and they were not wearing anything at all. Nobody took any notice of the group on the edge of the forest, for they were far too interested in what was happening in their midst. A man, who was wearing the brightest red sheepskin of all and who had a wide yellow-brown bracelet on his arm, had seized a boy by one ear and was shaking him backwards and forwards. The boy, who was about Edward's age but not so tall, was hopping from foot to foot and shouting:

'It wasn't my fault, honestly it wasn't!'

His voice had an unfamiliar accent, a little like that of Herr Braun who taught German at Edward's school twice a week.* But whatever language he was speaking, Meg and Edward understood perfectly, which was undoubtedly due to the kindly foresight of the Common which had in its time absorbed many languages and many ways of life.

'Oh, yes, it was,' the man said, shaking the boy harder than ever. 'The trouble with you is you just don't look what you're doing half the time.'

'That's exactly what Grandfather said to me about the brass polish,' whispered Edward. Which only goes to show that 2,500 years doesn't change human nature as much as you might think.

'Ow, leggo,' said the boy, 'you're hurting.'

'I'll hurt you some more in a minute,' the man growled, 'careless young idiot. How are we going to do the ploughing, eh? Answer me *that*!'

'Ed, Ed, Ed,' crowed Tommy, waving his rattle at the butterfly which had followed them out of the forest. The ox seemed to like the sound of the rattle. It opened its mouth and uttered a very loud noise halfway between a moo and a yawn. At this everybody in the village stopped telling the boy what they thought of him and turned round to look at the newcomers. There was a moment's silence during which Edward got ready to use the spectacles and then the boy let out a shout.

* This particular tribe had only arrived from the Rhineland a few generations ago.

'It's Mika, it is, it is. There you see, he's not lost at all. I told you he'd come home safely.'

And he twisted away from the man and came running lightly towards the ox who began to gallop in a clumsy, swaying manner to meet him. The boy threw his arms round the ox's neck—or as far as he could get them—and then pulled himself up on to its broad back and raised his hands clasped together in a boxer's salute.

'They do look *quite* friendly, don't they?' Meg asked, a shade nervously.

'Not too bad,' agreed Edward. 'Don't worry, we can always get out quickly if we have to. Come on and smile. Grandfather says that a cheerful smile and a cup of tea can solve most problems.'

By the time the two parties met, the smiles had become rather like fixed grins, and at least two hearts were beating very rapidly indeed, but the man with the wide bracelet seemed to be equally nervous which made Edward feel braver.

'Who are you and where do you come from?' the man asked.

'We're friends and we come from—from over there,' said Edward, waving towards the forest. It seemed pointless to try and explain about Farthing Row.

'From a large village?' the man demanded, still looking rather uncertain.

Meg was about to say 'enormous' because the population of Greater London was without doubt about five hundred thousand times as big as this place, but Edward got there first.

'No, even smaller than this,' he said, thinking only of Numbers One to Six.

'Even *smaller*?' said the man, bridling. 'This is a very *big* village. A very important village and *I* am the most important person in it, as I am the Headman.'

Several people said, 'Hear, hear' and 'That's right', and the man folded his arms and looked extremely pleased with himself. It occurred to Edward that his expression was very like that of one of the men who had come to see his grandfather on one of those secret business conferences. Edward hadn't liked him much either, but he wisely kept his thoughts to himself and only bowed.

'They did bring back Mika, father,' said the boy who had now ridden up to them. 'Not that Mika wouldn't have come home before dark, of course, but it is nice to have him back early.' And he gave Edward the shadow of a wink.

'Yes, yes, that is true,' agreed the Headman, stroking his beard. 'We thank you for that.'

'Not at all,' Edward murmured politely.

Most of the villagers had now managed to sidle round them in a circle and one of the women timidly stretched out a hand towards Tommy who waved his rattle and then began to bite on it.

'Is he teething, poor lamb?' asked the woman.

'Yes,' said Meg, 'he'll put anything in his mouth.'

'I know how it is,' the woman said, nodding, 'they all do it. A bronze necklace or a pig's trotter— anything so long as it's hard.'

'Ahem,' said the Headman, 'please do not interrupt while I am talking. Tell me, boy, why do you visit us? Have you come to trade? You appear to have some unusual objects about you.' And he fixed his gaze upon Edward's spectacles in a way that suddenly made Edward feel extremely uneasy.

'Yes,' he said quickly, 'we are—er—traders.'

'You seem rather young for the job,' said a voice from the crowd.

'We—we were chosen for our learning and knowledge,' gabbled Edward and added with a sudden stroke of brilliance, 'We wish to trade our goods for some of *your* learning.'

'No we don't,' objected Meg, who had just remembered that there was still some shopping in the bottom of the pram for which she would have to account to her mother.

'Yes, we do, shut up,' hissed Edward. 'Will you trade with us?' he asked the Headman who was now staring at Tommy's pram with rapt attention.

'We might, we might,' he said absently, 'that is a very fine carriage. Is the child of great importance?'

As Meg had always been rather ashamed of the shabbiness of the pram, which had been passed on third hand through various relations, she took a second look at it to see if it had changed. But the chrome was still peeling off and the long scratches on the side of the bodywork remained.

'Of very, very great importance,' said Edward, seeing another advantage. 'He is—is a Tommy and that is his magic sceptre.'

At these words absolute silence descended and then everybody, including the Headman, scrambled down on to their knees and even the boy on the ox shut his eyes tight.

'Ed, Ed, Ed,' said Tommy, taking the rattle out of his mouth and shaking it violently. Edward thought of saying that those were magic words, but decided he might be pushing his luck too far, so he only nodded solemnly.

'We'll trade,' said the Headman, getting back to his feet and brushing down his knees. 'Come this way please.' If Edward had been a little older and wiser in the ways of the world he might have distrusted the manner in which the Headman had suddenly become so friendly and meek, but he only put it down to his own cleverness and was so pleased with himself that he didn't notice that the Headman was talking out of the corner of his mouth to one of his followers.

'If we can separate the boy and the girl from the Important Tommy,' he muttered, 'we may well be able to learn his magic which will make us even more powerful. Tell my Number Two Wife that I have appointed her chief slave to the little one. She's good with babies, even if they have got magic powers. I will see that my son Oofa becomes friends with the other two. Go on, hop it, double quick.'

The man bowed and slithered away into the crowd, and the Headman turned and smiled at Edward and rubbed his hands together. He was not really a greedy or a bad man, but he was full of his own importance and he enjoyed throwing his weight about. Also he didn't fancy the idea of having to bow down to a boy who was the same age as his own son.

'Welcome, welcome,' he said as they reached the second largest hut, which was about the same size as Edward's bedroom at home. It was very dark inside after the bright sunshine, and the smell was a great deal stronger and far more unpleasant than it had been in the forest. Three piglets rushed between Edward's legs and he got a dreadful scare when he saw two bright yellow eyes glaring at him from the shadows. Then he saw the outline of two horns and a straggly beard and realized that it was only a goat. Meg didn't care for the inside of the Headman's hut and Tommy disliked it even more and said so extremely loudly.

The Number Two Wife, who was the woman who had spoken to Meg, had been given her orders and she now hurried forward, bowing as she advanced.

'Perhaps I could be of help?' she suggested timidly.

In spite of her long and rather dirty hair and the smudges of dust on her face and clothes she had a very nice, quite pretty face and she was only a few years older than Meg so, after a moment's hesitation while she rocked the pram up and down, Meg nodded and the Number Two Wife very gingerly put her hands on the chrome bar and very, very cautiously indeed, pulled Tommy back into the open air.

'I'd better go, too,' said Meg, starting to follow them, but the Headman raised his hand in horror.

'No, no,' he protested, 'you are our most honoured guests, please stay here. The Important Tommy will be well looked after, I promise you.'

'Well,' said Meg, 'I did tell moth—that is someone that I'd keep my eye on him.'

'He will be all right with me,' said the Number Two Wife from the doorway where she was making clucking noises at Tommy who had started to smile again.

'And you won't give him any bronze or bones or anything?' asked Meg. 'He—he prefers his magic rat-er-sceptre.'

'I would not dare to touch his magic rat-er-sceptre,' said the Number Two Wife in surprise.

'He'll be OK,' said Edward, who was longing to get on with the business in hand, so Meg reluctantly watched Tommy being pushed out of sight between the huts and turned back into the shadowy darkness.

'Sit down, sit down,' said the Headman, motioning to a long wooden stool. 'This is my son Oofa who will take my place one day, if he has learnt to guard the ox properly. It won't be for a long time naturally, not until I am an old, old man of some forty summers.'

'That's not old at all,' said Meg, whose own father was that age. 'Why, where we come from it's still thought of as quite young. I mean you don't get your pension until you're sixty-five.'

The Headman looked at her in a way which showed that he didn't understand a word of what she had said, but was trying to be polite. He transferred his attention to Edward who had been rapidly trying to think up some questions.

'Now then,' he said, 'what will you trade?'

'You tell me what I want to know first and then I'll show you,' said Edward cautiously. The Headman put back his head and roared with laughter.

'You are as cunning as the fox,' he said admiringly. 'Come, we will trade and trade about. What do you wish to know first?'

'How long has the village been here?' asked Edward.

'The summer sun must have risen and fallen a thousand times and all this while a village has rested here.'

'As long as that?' said Edward, doing some rapid mental arithmetic at which he was rather good. After all, Miss Witcham had told him they were going to start at the very beginning of the Common's history.

'Well since the days of my great-grandfather,' said the Headman rather crossly. 'We always add a few years, it impresses visiting neighbours. He cleared the trees and the undergrowth, but I had most of the huts built. It's no fun living in a forest, too damp for one thing, and then there are the wolves. That was two questions you know. Come on—trade?'

And he held out his hand. Edward searched frantically in the pocket of his jeans and finally brought out a large elastic band. He always carried a few around with him.

'That's not much,' the Headman said, peering at it.

'Just you wait and see,' said Edward and he felt

round on the dirt floor and found a small stone. He made the elastic into a catapult between his fingers and fitted in the stone.

'See that pot outside the door,' he said. 'Well, watch.'

He took careful aim and then let fly and the stone zinged out of the hut and hit the pot which, as it was only made of sun-dried mud, shattered into pieces. There was a moment's silence and the Headman wiped his forearm across his forehead and muttered:

'That is indeed magic. What is it called?'

'A guided missile,' Edward replied promptly. It sounded far grander than catapult, and it certainly impressed the Headman and his followers and Oofa, for they all repeated the words solemnly.

'Next question,' said Edward, who was starting to enjoy himself. 'Who gave you the right to settle here? I mean it's common land isn't it?'

'Right?' said the Headman, frowning. 'Why, the right of having the best flint arrows, the best swords, the best spears and the best axes of course. *We* have *socketed* axes, you know. No other village can stand against them, and as for it being common land – which was another double question, you know, so I shall expect two trades – why all land is common to all people. He who can take shall have. Surely you know *that*.'

And out came his hand again; only this time Edward had grown a little more cunning, too, and he took his time about finding the next object. There was his pen-knife – but it was rather a good one with three blades (one half broken) so he decided to hang on to it – a red biro, and a Southern Region timetable for last year.

'Come on, come on,' said the Headman, who was getting less and less respectful in spite of the rubber band.

Edward reluctantly handed over the biro and the Headman said:

'It's two questions you owe me for, don't forget,' so Edward had to produce the timetable as well. Everybody crowded round to have a look, and nobody noticed when a man slid silently into the hut and whispered in the Headman's ear.

'And what do they do?' the Headman asked.

'They make magic spells,' replied Edward and wrote on the paper, 'I think we'd better go now' and showed it to Meg. He had nothing else in his pockets except a very dirty handkerchief and he didn't think it would impress the villagers much. Also he had begun to realize that the atmosphere was growing rather uneasy.

'So do I,' said Meg. 'That is, it's a terribly strong spell and it shows us that it's time for us to go home.'

The Headman picked up the paper and held it close to his face and then turned it upside down; then he sniffed it and tasted the writing end of the biro. It had an unpleasant taste, of course, and the Headman spat hastily and rose to his feet.

'No, no,' he said. 'You can't leave yet, I wouldn't hear of it. You must rest here with the Important Tommy until your people come for you. This way we shall learn more of your magic. We have a special hut prepared for you.'

All the others rose to their feet, too, and somehow Edward and Meg found themselves being pushed out into the open where the shadows were already lengthening across the trodden earth, and the forest was turning a deep indigo colour. It was a very beautiful evening, with the smoke going straight up from a big bonfire which had been lit in the centre of the village, so that the women could start cooking the evening meal. But neither Meg nor Edward were in the mood to appreciate it as they were bundled into the largest hut of all, and before they realized what was happening, their hands were seized and tied very tightly indeed with strips of hide.

'Here, what are you doing?' asked Edward, struggling furiously.

The Headman folded his arms and looked even more self-important than usual.

'I am even *more* cunning than the fox,' he said. 'Your people will pay a good price for the Important Tommy and his magic rat-er-sceptre. They may even pay something for you. Tomorrow when the sun rises we will talk again. Sleep well.'

'But look here...' shouted Edward.

'Tommy, where's Tommy?' shouted Meg even louder.

'He is well. We always treat our prisoners well. We are not barbarians you know,' the Headman said, and the door shut behind him and a piece of wood was put across it from the outside. The sound of voices died away to a murmur and Edward and Meg were left alone in the darkness, prisoners in Bronze Age Britain and with no way of escaping unless they left Tommy behind.

'I wish we hadn't come,' whispered Meg. 'I want to go home.'

'Don't worry,' said Edward, who was more worried than he had ever been in his life, 'I'll think of something. And, anyway, don't forget we've got the Common on our side. It's sure to help.'

But even as he spoke he crossed his fingers behind his back, because what could the Common possibly do to get them out of this?

6. *The Gift*

IN SPITE of their dreadful anxiety both Edward and Meg must have dozed off, for Edward suddenly jerked upright as he heard a scuffling sound right behind him. For one awful moment he thought it might be a rat or even a wolf, but then a voice said in a low whisper:

'Psst, are you awake? It's me, Oofa.'

'What do you want?' Edward whispered back.

'I came to see if I could help, bring you some food or something. You did find Mika for me and one good turn deserves another and all that.'

'Couldn't you get us out?' Edward asked.

'How? All I've got is one of father's old axe-heads and it's dreadfully blunt. Couldn't you magic yourselves free?'

'Not without Tommy,' Edward said gloomily. 'If only I had—hold on a minute, why didn't I think of that before! Here, Meg, Meg.'

'Wassit?' Meg's voice said sleepily. 'Oh, where am I?

'In the big hut. Don't make a noise. Listen, if I shuffle over to you, could you get my knife out of my pocket? Just keep talking so I know where you are—but quietly.'

It wasn't an easy thing to do but, after a lot of muttering and 'look out, that was nearly my eye', Meg managed to find the knife and between them they got the biggest blade opened; and then Meg held the handle as firmly as she could and Edward pushed his bound wrists backwards and forwards across it. And the knife, being a very good one, soon made short work of the cowhide thongs. Then it was Meg's turn to be set free and after they had rubbed their wrists they crawled over to the crack in the planks which Oofa was doing his best to make bigger. The knife came in very handy again and Edward used the broken blade as a lever to get the plank loose until he could swing it sideways.

'Come on,' Oofa whispered, 'there's nobody about, they're all asleep except me.'

There was quite a lot of heavy snoring going on – even the ox, now extra firmly tethered, was snorting in the middle of the pathway. It was a warm, moonless night but the starlight was bright enough to see by and some of the embers were still glowing.

'Where's Tommy?' demanded Meg, catching hold of Oofa's skinny little arm and shaking it.

'He sleeps in the hut of my father and his number two wife,' Oofa replied. 'You'll never get him out without waking them up.'

'We've got to try,' Edward said.

Oofa peered at him in the starlight and saw the reflection of the dying fire in Edward's spectacles.

'Tell me, why do you have Four Eyes?' he said hesitantly.

Edward stiffened, but Meg said quickly:

'It's because he's so clever.'

A remark which suddenly made Edward determined to get them all out of this situation somehow. But how? What he had remembered about the knife being in his pocket had saved them before, so perhaps they had other hidden weapons too.

'What's in the pram?' he whispered.

'Tommy of course – oh, his rattle, sceptre I mean, and a spare nappy, and a library book, and a packet of salt, and a tin of baked beans for supper, if we ever get any supper,' and her voice trembled, 'and some fizzy lemon. I think that's all. Oh, my hair-slide because it came off. Why?'

Edward frowned deeply, it wasn't much of a collection in the way of weapons, but there must be something there that might help. A water pistol now or, even better, a twenty-five pence rocket would be perfect and in future he could see he would have to plan things properly. The fire sank lower with a sudden crackle which made them all jump and jolted Edward's brain into action.

'Show me where the pram is,' he said to Oofa, 'the – the carrying stool in which the Important Tommy rides. Meg, you stay here and don't move!'

Meg stood like a ramrod in the shadows by the hut, with just her eyes following Edward and Oofa as they went down on all fours and crept into the hut of the Headman, who was snoring so loudly it was a wonder he didn't wake himself up – and everybody else into the bargain. Very, very gently Edward stepped over the sleeping figures and put his hand inside the pram basket and felt around until his fingers closed over what he wanted. He was just making the return journey when the Headman gave an extra loud snort and said quite plainly.

'Not barbarians,' and then turned over and went to sleep again. Edward blew out his cheeks noiselessly and tiptoed out to where Meg was now holding on to Oofa for support.

'Now listen,' Edward whispered, 'I'm going to do something very, very magical in a minute and everybody will come rushing out to see – everybody. As soon as that happens Meg and I are going into your father's hut and we are going to vanish with the Important Tommy.'

'Oh my,' breathed Oofa, his eyes wide with astonishment. 'Although I'm sorry you're going really. I was going to let you ride Mika if they didn't keep you prisoners.'

'Yes, that's a pity,' agreed Edward, 'but look here, aren't you going to get into awful trouble for helping us?'

'Nobody will ever know,' Oofa replied. 'I share a hut with six of my younger brothers and they'd never dare to split on me. Anyway they won't know because I shall run to watch the magic like everybody else. Will it be frightening?'

'It will be astonishing,' Edward promised. 'You've been jolly kind and I'd like to give you something to show that we're not barbarians either. Here, take this. It's better than your old axe.' And he handed over the pocket-knife which is how iron was first introduced to that particular settlement, making them very superior towards their neighbours who were still using bronze and flint.

'I say, *thanks*,' said Oofa. 'But you're not supposed to give a weapon without getting something in return, otherwise it will cut the bond of friendship. Here,' and in his turn he handed over a very thin bracelet which Edward accepted politely, although he knew of course that he could never wear it.

'Now then,' he said, bracing himself. 'Meg, stand back in the shadows, and you Oofa. Are you ready? Then here goes.' And at the top of his lungs Edward shouted:

'Two, Four, Six, Eight.
Whom do we appreciate?
Fulham UNITED!'

By the time he started chanting this again most of the village, sleepy-eyed and bewildered, were running towards the open space in front of the Headman's hut, and even the ox had slowly begun to get to its feet, shaking its enormous horns from side to side, and the sheep, goats and pigs were adding to the din of raised voices.

'Behold!' bellowed Edward, holding something above

his head, 'I the Mighty Four-Eyes am free and about to make some great magic. Watch, you will never have seen anything like it in your lives before. There will be a great blue flame and we shall vanish back to our own village for ever.'

And as he finished speaking Edward tore open the top of the packet and threw the contents on to the fire. For one terrible moment nothing happened and then the fire roared upwards, no longer red but blue, just as Edward had said it would be.

A great 'OOOO-AAAAA' went up from the crowd and then they all, even the Headman, fell flat on their faces and at the same time Edward seized Meg's hand and pulled her into the hut and clasped hold of Tommy's warm little hand.

'Shut your eyes, shut your eyes, shut your eyes, I'm going to wish...' he cried.

'No, no, no,' Meg said, tugging one hand free.

'I'm wishing,' Edward persisted in an agony of impatience as the blue flames began to die down.

'Wait,' said Meg, and she rushed back into the open and pushed something into the cold and trembling hand of the Number Two Wife and whispered, 'It's for you, a present for looking after Tommy.'

And then, just in time, for the Headman was getting to his feet, Meg raced back to Edward and clasped hands, and as the whirling mist gathered round them, Edward caught a glimpse of the Headman in the doorway, his hand gripping an axe which he was holding above his head...Then he had gone, blotted out by the floating coloured clouds, and the growing roar of voices vanished too, and all they could hear was quite a different kind of roar as a motorbike came round Farthing Lane much too fast.

'That was a jolly silly thing to do,' said Edward, who

was very pale, 'you nearly messed the whole thing up. They might have captured us again.'

'It was my plastic hairslide,' said Meg, sinking down on to the grass. 'I thought she'd like it to keep her hair out of her eyes.'

There was a long, long silence while they got their breath back. Travelling across two and a half thousand years takes a bit of getting used to, and the familiar Common still seemed strange.

'Do you realize,' Edward said at last, 'that we're right bang in the middle of the Headman's hut?'

'Don't,' said Meg and shivered. 'Oh what have they done to Tommy? He's got blue paint all over his poor little face.'

'Woad I expect,' Edward said absently—'Oofa had some on his arms. I say, we're not back where we started. We *started* in the front garden and now we're on the other side of the road.'

'Well we walked it, silly,' said Meg, 'the Row is in the middle of the forest. At least it was—no it is—well it should be—I think. Tommy, hold still, I want to clean your face.'

'I suppose we *did* go,' Edward said. 'I mean, we couldn't have imagined it all could we?'

And then he felt the thin bracelet in his pocket and he also noticed that lying at the bottom of the pram were some rather wilting, but most unusual blue flowers with a very strong, sweet smell.

'Crikey!' said Edward. 'Here, you can have this bracelet thing. It was jolly nice of Oofa to give it to me, but I wouldn't half get teased at school if I wore it and I get teased enough as it is,' and he sighed slightly. 'Well, we know one thing. At least the answer wasn't there, not unless we're going to defend the Row with axes and spears and things. We'll just have to try again.'

'Not yet we won't,' Meg said firmly. 'Bother this stuff, it won't come off at all. Edward, how did you make the fire turn blue?'

'Cooking salt,' said Edward simply. 'I learnt about it in school. It's funny how learning things does come in useful sometimes. I'm sorry all the salt's gone; we'll have to buy some more. Have you got any money? I haven't.'

'No,' said Meg shortly. She was tired and getting cross and she wanted to do something very ordinary and safe like cooking the baked beans or watching television. As they reached the edge of the Row, Miss Rose Witcham came hurrying towards them looking very anxious.

'You've been gone a lot longer than five minutes,' she said, 'more like fifteen. What?'

'We'd walked a bit,' said Edward. 'It wasn't any good. Those Bronze Age people just took what they wanted, they didn't believe in rights and Common land and all that.'

'Dear me,' Miss Rose said, frowning, 'so it was a wasted journey, was it?'

There was a short pause and then Edward replied.

'No, not really, it was quite fun in a way and jolly interesting. Seeing how people lived and all that and some of them were quite nice.'

'And some of them were quite nasty,' Meg added. She was still trying to get the woad off Tommy's face without much success, and that meant she'd have two things to explain away to her mother, woad and salt.

'Perhaps you'd care for some lemonade and biscuits?' suggested Miss Rose, who now realized that Edward and Meg were not in the best of spirits. 'And I should like the opportunity to hear of some of your travels if you'd be kind enough to tell me them. It would be like old times.'

'Very old times,' said Edward drily. He started laughing and after a moment Meg joined in and lost her crossness. She had never been inside the front room of Number One before, and her reactions were very much the same as Edward's had been when she saw the rocking-horse and the chest and the kite, not to mention the white kitten which was cleaning its ears on the window-sill. Miss Lily was sitting at a large table that was entirely covered with books, and her eyebrows rose hopefully as she saw the visitors standing in the doorway. Miss Rose shook her head and Miss Lily said:

'Well it was too much to hope that anyone could succeed at the *first* attempt. Edward, if you would care to move those chairs and that screen to one side, I believe Tommy would be more comfortable out of his pram.'

'He probably would,' agreed Meg, 'but he might hurt your things.'

'It doesn't matter if he does,' said Miss Rose, going off towards the kitchen. 'My sister can always mend.'

So Tommy was put down on the rug and was soon crawling about tasting this and that and talking to himself.

'I see,' said Miss Lily, 'that he has been sampling some Isatis Tinctoria already.'

'He's what?' Meg asked in alarm.

'My sister means,' said Miss Rose, returning with a laden tray, 'woad. It's really only a yellow flower, quite pretty too. I tried to grow some in our garden, but it needs a chalky soil and we're gravel on the Common. It won't hurt him, which reminds.'

'But I can't get it off,' Meg interrupted. 'I've scrubbed and scrubbed with a handkerchief but it hasn't made any difference.'

'Poor lamb,' said Miss Rose, exactly as the Number Two Wife had done. 'Never mind. I think I have a little something in the kitchen that will do the trick. Which reminds.'

But she had gone before they knew what it was she kept being reminded about. However, when she returned a few moments later she had with her not only a plastic pot with some pink cream in it, but also one of the now very wilting blue flowers.

'Look, Lily,' she exclaimed, 'Endymion non-scripta pura. Here, Meg dear, the woad-remover,' and she handed over the pink cream.

'End-y what?' asked Edward.

'Bluebell, but a very early species. That's what they used to be like, but of course you know that. I suppose – I suppose you wouldn't sell it to me?'

'Gosh, we wouldn't *sell* them,' said Edward. 'We picked them free – at least Meg did.'

Meg looked up from where she was cleaning Tommy's face which was now only blue in parts. She hesitated and then said:

'Could – could I trade them, all of them, for some salt? A whole packet if you've got one. Would that be mean?'

'Not mean at all,' said Miss Rose, 'very wise. Two-way gifts always make one feel so much better somehow.'

'That's exactly what Oofa said,' put in Edward and that, of course, led very naturally to the whole of the story of the village which the two Miss Witchams enormously enjoyed.

'Oh doesn't it take one back?' sighed Miss Rose. 'There's nothing like travel for broadening the mind, and time travel is the best kind of all for getting to understand people.'

'Sometimes a bit too well,' said Edward, rubbing his wrists which were still a bit sore. 'It's a pity it didn't do any good.'

'Which brings me to the next point,' said Miss Lily. 'I've been doing quite a lot of reading and I feel that about the 1300s (AD I hasten to add) might be a good time. It's no good fussing about with the Romans or William the Conqueror because everything was so topsy-turvy then, but by the fourteenth century or so matters were settling down. What do you feel about it, Edward?'

'Me?' said Edward uneasily as he finished off the last of the biscuits. 'Well – er, um...'

'Not right away, naturally,' said Miss Rose soothingly as she filled his lemonade glass. 'You're sure to want a rest. But time *is* running short. We had a visitor today and.'

'He went to call on your parents after us, Meg,' said Miss Lily. 'I told him there would be nobody at home, but he would go. He's that kind of person.'

'What visitor?' asked Meg. Tommy's face was now back to its normal pink and he was enjoying himself rocking the wooden cradle backwards and forwards.

'Him,' said Miss Lily, pointing out of the window with one bent finger.

A man was standing by the garden gate busily writing in a small notebook. He was of medium height and getting a little stout and he hadn't got a beard, but Edward and Meg recognized him instantly.

'It's the Headman,' whispered Edward, and Meg cowered back on the hearthrug and clutched Tommy.

'That's exactly how he behaves,' agreed Miss Lily, nodding, 'only these days he calls himself the Council Rehousing Officer. He's been to see your grandfather twice, Edward. He wants to put us all into a new block of flats on an Estate. We've told him that we don't intend to go but he doesn't take any notice. Well?'

There was a silence, which was broken only by the thudding of the rocking cradle and the rumble of the traffic down the main road. Edward took a deep breath.

'Tell us more about the 1300s,' he said.

7. *The Second Journey*

It was unanimously decided that a few days' rest were needed in which to plan the next expedition. Both Edward and Meg felt somewhat nervous after their experience with the Headman and his followers, but strangely enough these unpleasant memories soon grew less important while the friendliness of the Number Two Wife and Oofa remained. All the same, Edward did get a bit of a fright one afternoon when he was busily making out a list of 'trades' to take with him on the next journey. He was so engrossed in what he was doing that he didn't even hear the door open until his grandfather said sharply:

'On your feet, boy, on your feet.'

And there, standing in the doorway behind the Commander was the Headman-Rehousing Officer. Edward jumped to attention all right, but the man only smiled and rubbed his hands and said:

'So you're Edward, are you? And how are we today? Working hard I see!'

'Yes,' mumbled Edward, trying to cover up the list and only succeeding in spilling his papers on the floor.

'That's good, that's good,' said the Rehousing Officer. 'I like to see a boy working, it shows he means to get on in the world.'

'Humph,' said the Commander, glaring fiercely from underneath his white eyebrows, 'not much of a world for a youngster to grow up *in*, if you ask me, when half the time he can't do anything without getting official permission.'

'Now, now,' said the Rehousing Officer, 'that's not the right attitude to take, Mr Hobson, and...'

'Commander Hobson,' barked the Commander.

'Ah yes, of course, *Commander* Hobson. Well as I was saying, it's all for your own good, you know. We can't do exactly as we please about everything, we have to fit in with the community. I am quite sure that you and Edward will thoroughly enjoy living on the Estate. You'll have every modern convenience, central heating, a waste-disposal chute, constant hot water and, of course, no stairs,' and he beamed at the Commander whose face went bright puce at the insinuation that he was too old to climb up the three flights which led to Edward's bedroom.

'And as for you, Edward,' the man went on, 'there will be other boys for you to make friends with, and a special playground in which you can run about and have plenty of exercise.'

'I like the Common,' said Edward, 'and we've got a garden, and I've already got friends. I've got Jellicoe and Meg and—and Tommy and Miss Lily and Miss Rose.'

The Rehousing man went on smiling exactly as if he hadn't heard a word that Edward had said.

'That reminds me,' he said, wagging one finger. 'Jellicoe is, I understand, your dog. Naturally we don't allow animals on the Estate, so he will have to be put down. However, as he is not as young, shall we say, as he was, this may well be a blessing in disguise.'

Edward glanced in horror at his grandfather who looked away, and from that moment Edward knew that he would rather be captured by pirates or thrown into the darkest dungeon than be made to lose Farthing Row and Jellicoe.

'We don't want to go and we shan't,' he said loudly.

But the Rehousing Officer had picked up the paper off the floor and was reading the list.

'Knife, fireworks, matches, packet soup, alarm clock, coloured biros, paper, clockwork train, fizzy lemon, bicycle bell!' he read. 'Is this some kind of memory game you're playing?'

'Yes, sort of,' Edward agreed.

'Very instructive,' the Rehousing man said. 'Well, I must be on my way, I have a lot of work to attend to myself. My department is a very busy one you know, and I have a great deal of responsibility. Goodbye, Edward. Come along, Commander.'

He bustled out and Edward's grandfather said in a low voice:

'Insufferable fellow. I'd like to have had him under *my* command for a bit. I'd have knocked some of the bounce out of him. Look here, boy, about Jellicoe. I'm sorry. Can't say more than that. But I know, I know...'

'We're *not* going,' Edward said passionately. 'None of us, ever. I won't let it happen. I won't!'

His grandfather looked surprised at this unusual behaviour on the part of his normally quiet grandson, and he put his hand on Edward's shoulder for a moment and said:

'Good to hear you talk like that, didn't know you had it in you, boy, but you can't fight progress, if progress you can call it. Oh, I'm coming, I'm coming.'

And he stumped off in answer to the impatient call of the Rehousing Officer. Edward screwed up the list into a ball and chucked it at the wall and then slowly went and picked it up, and smoothed it out, and went back to work. The trouble was he thought of so many things that he couldn't get them all into his pockets, and he had to pack some of them in a carrier-bag with Marks and Spencer on the side of it. When he met Meg on the morning which they had decided would be THE one, he saw that she had had the same problem for Tommy's pram basket was crammed full, added to which Meg was wearing a great deal of plastic jewellery.

'It's all old stuff,' she said. 'I use it for dressing up and all that. This ring came out of a cracker and so did the bracelet, and I got the bubble-blowing stuff in my stocking last Christmas. I don't think it's gone off.'

She was talking a lot because she was nervous.

'Well, we should be jolly well all right this time,' Edward said a great deal more cheerfully than he felt, because he was scared too; only of course he couldn't show it in front of Meg. So he tied up the laces of his plimsolls in a double knot, put the carrier-bag on the loaded pram, took hold of the hands of Meg and Tommy and wished. They had decided to travel from the back garden of Number Six, as it was early closing day and there were quite a lot of people out on the Common enjoying the sunshine, and as Edward had pointed out, it might lead to some awkward questions if the three of them vanished while somebody was looking...

The raspberry canes were swallowed up by the swirling mist and the coloured clouds drifted round them and then cleared and, before he saw anything else at all, Edward was aware of the noise. There were people laughing and talking and shouting at one another. There were animals grunting and mooing and cackling. Several musical instruments were being played both loudly and rather out of tune, and there was a lot of water splashing. It made Edward think of the fun-fair at Battersea Park, and as his vision cleared he saw why—the three of them were standing on the edge of a fairground.

'What is it?' asked Meg in a trembling voice with her eyes still screwed tightly shut.

'It's all right,' Edward replied. 'It's nice. Go on—look.'

And it was certainly well worth looking at! The whole of the Common was covered with booths and sideshows and tables piled high with goods, from rabbit skins to mounds of apples, from woven materials to pieces of leather, from ornaments to saddles. And to one side there were rough wooden wickets which were supposed to contain horses, sheep, cows, pigs, ducks, geese and hens. But quite a number of the animals had managed to slip free and were now wandering about, getting trampled on, and adding to the general uproar.

Most of the people were dressed in very simple clothes of linen or wool. The men wore hooded tunics which came to just below the knee and stockings and boots or soft leather shoes, and some of them had no shoes at all. And the women wore long, rather loosely fitting dresses which reached to the ground. Their hair was bound round with linen caps or scarves, although the girls had long plaits. Edward couldn't help smiling when he saw that grown-up, even elderly men as well as boys, wore their hair down to their shoulders. It was a pity his grandfather wasn't here to see this, because he was always muttering about the disgusting modern fashion of young men not cutting their hair. Apparently it wasn't modern at all, only very old-fashioned.

A few people were dressed in much grander clothes made of silk and velvet and one old man who was standing quite close to them was wearing a fur bonnet on his head and a long robe with a very full skirt that reminded the open-mouthed Meg of her mother's dressing-gown. It was Edward who noticed that the old man's belt was studded with jewels which sent out brilliant flashes of coloured light as the sun caught them.

There was so much to see that Edward and Meg were quite content just to stand and watch for a while. On the far side of the Common were some trees and beyond them the land dipped downwards to a broad valley. Edward, with the help of his spectacles, was able to make out the glint of water which he supposed was the Thames, although it seemed to be much wider than the river he knew. There was also a faint cloud of mist—or it could have been smoke—hanging over it, but no houses at all.

'Look behind us,' whispered Meg, pinching his arm.

There were three tiny cottages with wooden walls and thatched roofs and it seemed to Edward that although eighteen centuries had passed since he was here last methods of building hadn't improved very much. The cottages only had two windows apiece, but there was no glass in them, only broad wooden shutters at the sides which were now fastened back against the walls. The smoke had to find its way out into the open through a hole in the roof. An old woman was sitting by the doorway of the cottage nearest to them, her bent fingers working at surprising speed as she pulled at pieces of what appeared to be grey cottonwool and turned them into long threads. She smiled and nodded as she caught Edward's eye and after a moment's hesitation he went over to her.

'Lovely day for the fair, isn't it?' she said. 'Have you come far?'

'From over there,' said Edward vaguely.

'You'll be foreigners then?'

'Oh no, we're English.'

'Foreigners,' she repeated stubbornly. 'If you're not born in this parish then you're a foreigner, but welcome just the same.'

'Please what are you doing?' Meg asked.

'Carding fleece from the sheep. Don't you have sheep in your village?'

'No,' Meg said regretfully.

'Must be a poor place.'

'It's not at all—just different,' Meg said.

'I've travelled a bit myself,' the old woman boasted, 'I went to London once.'

'But this is London—isn't it?' asked Edward.

'Bless you, no.' The old woman stopped working and

burst into a cackle of laughter. 'London's a great big city with shops and houses and boats and churches, although I don't remember it too well, to tell the truth. Get off, get off, off I say!' This last remark was addressed to a large sow which was waddling towards them, grunting and puffing, her little piggy eyes glistening as she saw a white cat come out of the cottage. The cat arched its back and spat and the sow came to a halt.

'Jack,' the old woman shouted. 'Bring Bessie here or we'll have trouble.'

A boy appeared in the doorway and put the cat on to the thatch out of harm's way. Then he whistled between his teeth and a goose suddenly waddled out of the darkness of the house towards the sow, flapping her wings and sticking out her neck and hissing. The sow gave a grunt and heaved herself off into the crowd. The goose preened her feathers and settled down on the grass.

'There's my Bessie,' the old woman said, 'she looks after me a treat. Better than a knight in full armour she is. Jack, here's a couple of young foreigners come to see our fair. This is Jack, my great nephew.'

'Hello,' the boy said, strolling over. He was taller than Edward and looked rather superior. 'I bet you haven't travelled as far as I have,' he went on. 'I've come from London.'

'There,' said the old woman, nodding, 'what do you think to that, eh? He's an apprentice, he is. Why don't you show them round, I don't expect that they have fairs as grand as this in their parts.'

'Yes, we do,' Edward said, stung by the way the boy was smiling at them. 'We've got Battersea Fun Fair.'

'Get on with you,' Jack replied, grinning more widely than ever, 'I know Battersea and it's nothing but an old marsh. I was there this morning as it happens because my Uncle and I travelled down from London by boat and we put ashore at Battersea. So there!'

'What are you apprenticed at?' asked Meg hurriedly as Edward began to grow rather red.

'Apprenticed to,' the boy corrected her. 'You don't know much, do you? I'm going to be a cordwainer.'

As neither Edward nor Meg had the faintest idea what this meant, and they didn't want to show any more ignorance, there was a pause during which Jack, his hands in his low-slung leather belt, led them into the fair.

'One day,' said Jack, 'I'll make shoes as fine as those,' and he pointed to the feet of a woman who was hurrying past with her skirts slightly raised, for the ground was covered in all kinds of refuse. Meg looked and then looked again, for the woman was wearing shoes almost identical to her own, with very thick wooden soles and just a wide band of leather over the front to keep them on.

'Yours aren't bad either,' said Jack grudgingly, 'even if the rest of your clothes are a bit dull.' It was Meg's turn to go red for she knew very well that her dress was too long for her and too large altogether, but she didn't think it compared too badly with what the other girls were wearing.

'Now look here,' said Edward, stopping short, 'there's no need to be so jolly rude all the time. If you don't want to show us round you don't have to.'

'All right, keep your hair on,' Jack said. 'What do you want to see first? There's the giant or the man with the two-headed calf, or you can have a go on the greasy pole over the pond, or...'

It was difficult to make a choice, there was so much to look at and all of it was interesting, and they had to keep stopping because Meg couldn't get the pram through the crowds. The pram and Edward's spectacles were, in fact, proving something of an embarrassment, and when he became aware that quite a number of children had started to follow them and to point and giggle he decided that something had to be done. He had a quick whispered conversation with Meg who only listened with half an ear as she stared enraptured at a stall where a woman in gaudy clothes was selling jewellery.

'Yes, I suppose so, isn't that pretty?' said Meg.

So Tommy was hauled out of the pram and put into his sister's arms. Wrapped in his shawl he looked astonishingly like every other baby on the Common, and Edward took off his glasses and put them in his pocket and then wheeled the pram back to the old woman who was now talking to a grey-haired man with very bright blue eyes.

'Well, I won't do it and that's final,' she was saying.

'But Aunty, it's not *safe*,' the man said with a worried frown.

'Safe? Nonsense. This cottage was good enough for my father and it's certainly good enough for me. Don't talk a lot of rubbish.'

The man sighed and smiled at Edward who had halted the pram.

'Please,' Edward said, 'please could you possibly look after this for us until we get back?'

'Yes, boy,' the old woman nodded, 'put it round the back, by the water butt. Funny sort of thing, one of these newfangled ideas I suppose. Like some others I could mention,' and she gave the man a scornful look and hobbled into the darkness of her home. There was a clattering and a squealing and a piglet dashed out of the front door and was sent on its way by the goose who gave it a playful nip as it scurried past.

'Newfangled or not,' the man said, studying the pram, 'I think it's very fine. May I push it for you? How well it rides too. What is that material with which the wheels are covered?'

'Rubber,' said Edward, foreseeing yet more difficulties.

'Rubber. Rubber—and where does that come from?'

'Trees I think. I'm not sure.'

'Oh, a type of bark, most interesting. And this hood, how does...'

'I'm awfully sorry,' said Edward, 'but I'm frightened I shall lose my friends in the crowd if I don't hurry.'

'Of course, of course.' The man abandoned the pram regretfully behind the rain tub and then went on, 'Perhaps I could come with you? Aunty told me a little about you—I'm her nephew by the way—Stephen the Scavenger.'

'You don't look like one,' said Edward kindly.

'Oh don't I?' said Mr Stephen, looking rather hurt as he was proud of his profession. 'Naturally I'm not wearing my badge of office as I'm not on duty, although sometimes I feel as though I'm never off it. Look at my aunt's house for instance. The danger of fire, I mean, but *she* won't see it. They never do until it's too late and the place has gone up in smoke. We're for ever having fires in London and we do try to make people put tiles on their roofs but they won't because of the cost and reeds and straw are so much cheaper. We keep fire-hooks hanging in the churches, but by the time the alarm's given it's ten to one it's too late to do much good.'

'What else do you do?' Edward asked. He had had no idea that Scavenging meant being a kind of fireman.

'You don't want to hear about my work,' Mr Stephen said, smiling.

'Oh yes I do, please.'

'Well, originally we were Customs men, but gradually the job spread to take in other work. We have to supervise cleaning the streets and that's no joke when people will keep on emptying rubbish out of the windows. We have to see that the pavements are kept in good condition and that nobody sets up a stall so that it blocks up the road, or hangs out a sign that would be in the way. And then there are the oyster fishermen who will fasten the ropes from their boats too high so that people trip over them. They're a real bunch of villains, those fishermen, you be careful if you ever come to London. Half the time the oysters they sell aren't fresh. We're always warning them, but it doesn't seem to make any difference.'

Edward took all this in, turned it over in his mind and said:

'So it's really a jolly important job, isn't it?'

'We Scavengers think it's a very *necessary* job,' Mr Stephen replied, 'and it's certainly interesting with London growing so fast these days. Some say that one day it may spread as far as the village of Westminster, but I think that's going too far myself. In a city as large as that no man would know more than his immediate neighbours and it would be a lonely kind of life. Besides, it'd make travelling such a business. The river would become jammed with traffic.'

Edward thought of the vast and sprawling London that he knew and was tempted to try to explain it to his companion.

'I'm sure it *will* grow bigger,' he said. 'There'll be houses and roads as far as you can see from the top of the tallest building and there'll be *millions* of people living there.'

Mr Stephen put back his head and laughed and then slapped Edward on the back.

'The whole population of England, in fact,' he said. 'Well, my young soothsayer, I hope you're wrong. I shouldn't care to live in such a place, I can tell you. Hallo, there's Jack.'

'Oh Edward, look!' exclaimed Meg, running up to him with Tommy in her arms. She held out her hand on all four fingers of which were large rings. 'Aren't they smashing? I swopped—traded them, I mean—for my plastic ones and the poppet beads.'

'But, but...' stuttered Edward, 'you can't do that. Those must be worth thousands of pounds.'

'They're not real,' Mr Stephen said, 'unfortunately for you. But they're very pretty all the same. And what a wise choice you've made. Let me see, you've got "diamonds" which will protect you from your enemies, "emeralds" that will make you rich and protect your eyes, "rubies" which will save you from poverty and "sapphires" that will give you great happiness.'

'There,' said Meg proudly, 'I think they're much nicer than real jewels because I won't have to worry about robbers and thieves and people.'

'Very wise,' agreed Mr Stephen. 'You see that man over there?' And he nodded towards the elderly gentleman they had noticed earlier. 'Now his stones *are* real. He's a very rich merchant and he always carries his wealth with him in his belt. Well, what do you wish to see next?'

Jack stopped showing off quite so much now that his uncle had joined the party, but he was still very happy to talk about himself given half a chance. He appeared to work quite hard but, he told Edward, he had a lot of fun too.

'We run races and when the Thames freezes over we go skating. I've made myself a splendid pair of skates out of bone and I can go like the wind, almost as fast as a galloping horse.'

'As a trotting horse perhaps?' corrected Mr Stephen, who was now carrying Tommy. Meg was feeling a bit tired.

'All right, trotting,' Jack lowered his voice. 'And we "put the stone" and have javelin throwing competitions and we have fights too with swords and bucklers, just like real knights. And we shoot the rapids.'

'Don't let your great-aunt Mag hear you say that,' said Mr Stephen, who had sharp ears, 'she'd have a fit.'

'But there aren't any rapids in the Thames,' objected Edward.

'Yes there are,' said Jack scornfully. 'You've never been to London, so you wouldn't know.'

'And just *you* mind your manners, my lad,' said his uncle. 'I expect Edward's been to a few places you haven't, so don't go thinking you know it all. There *are* rapids of a sort, Edward. Peter Colechurch, who was a really wonderful builder a hundred and fifty years ago, planned the London Bridge we have today. It took about thirty-three years to construct, and it's got a series of arches, twenty of 'em, and these stand on piers, which in turn are protected by starlings as we call them. They're man-made islands of stone and, when the tide turns, the water falls as much as five feet and rushes between these starlings *quite* as fast as a galloping horse. Some of these young lads think it's clever to try and sail a boat over these waterfalls. I don't think it's in the least clever because somebody's always getting drowned. If you *want* to get wet, Jack, have a try on the greasy pole over the pond!'

This shut Jack up for some rather sulky minutes, but he wasn't a bad boy at heart and when Edward read a notice which was pinned up by a booth, Jack's manner towards him changed to one of deep respect.

'Can you really read?' he asked admiringly, 'or did you make that up?'

'No, that's what it says,' Edward replied, rather pleased that at last he'd found something he could do which Jack could not. 'All stallholders' fees must be paid to the Lord of the Fair. Mr Stephen, is he the person who owns the Common?'

Excitement flickered in Edward's voice as he spoke. Could they have come at last to the right time and place to find out the answer to the problem of Farthing Row?

'No, no.' Mr Stephen shook his head and stopped to buy Tommy what looked like a stick of barley sugar, for that young gentleman was now trying to bite the clasp which fastened Mr Stephen's short cloak to his shoulders. Meg looked a little anxious, but Tommy seemed to like this new – or rather old – sweet and was soon dribbling happily. 'No,' Mr Stephen went on, 'the Common belongs to everyone. Each man can make use of a part of it, of course, for planting seeds or feeding his animals, or he may let it lie fallow for a while. But it doesn't actually belong to him. The Lord of the Fair is merely an officer or bailiff who's appointed by the local nobleman or city corporation, or who ever it may be, to see that the stallholders pay their rent. What a very serious person you are, Edward. You're going to be a real scholar one day.'

Edward smiled wanly as yet again he saw his chances of finding the elusive solution fade away. Like Meg he was beginning to feel a bit tired and the Marks and Spencer carrier-bag was starting to get very heavy. But the very next second he had no reason to complain about *that* for there were sudden running footsteps and heavy breathing, and then the bag was snatched from his hand by a small man dressed in green, who wriggled through a gap in the crowds and was away almost before Edward was able to shout.

'Stop thief! Stop – stop!' he cried desperately.

8. *Dick-the-Thief*

'CHEER up,' Mr Stephen said, 'we'll get your goods back for you soon enough, we usually do you know. I remember when there was that really bad affair when a great deal of property was stolen from our Abbey at Westminster, but it was all recovered in the end.'

'How long did it take?' Edward asked without much hope.

They had spent nearly two hours searching for the man in green, but he appeared to have got clean away and Edward's eyes, without their spectacles, were beginning to ache.

'Not long,' said Mr Stephen, shifting Tommy to the other arm very carefully so as not to wake him up, 'a couple of months perhaps. You'd better let me have a list of what you've had stolen.'

'Well there was—' said Edward and stopped rather like Miss Rose often did. How could he possibly explain a packet of dried vegetable soup and three Woolworth biros, not to mention a clockwork train?

'Well?' said Jack impatiently.

'Some, some food,' Edward said desperately, and—um, three pens and er—some parchment for writing on you know and a—er—toy and a bottle of very nice lemonade and a knife.'

'Quite valuable belongings,' agreed Mr Stephen, 'no wonder you're upset.'

They had walked right round the Fair, carefully avoiding the two-headed calf as neither Edward nor Meg had wanted to see that—although Jack had gone off to look—and were now nearing the three cottages where Aunty lived. They had crossed a very rutted track which Edward, even in his gloomy state, had been interested to realize would one day become the busy road that he knew. There had been very little traffic on it today however, only a small boy driving some sheep, a woman leading a pony and a man dressed in leather trousers and a rather frayed chainmail jerkin riding on an enormous shire horse.

'A Knight!' whispered Meg, quite forgetting that her feet hurt.

'Probably coming to see if he can buy a saddle second or third hand,' agreed Mr Stephen. 'They get sent in for refurbishing, but if they're in a very bad state the saddlemakers touch 'em up a bit to make them look all right and then resell them. It's not exactly illegal, but they do sail pretty close to the wind.'

To their left there was a little dip in the land and beyond that the thick trees of a forest with here and there a thin plume of smoke rising into the still, hot air to show where the charcoal burners were at work.

'Never mind,' said Edward, 'it can't be helped. It wasn't much really.'

'I should call it a great deal,' Mr Stephen said rather coldly. 'Naturally if your family is so rich that...' and then he stopped. They all did, for the most extraordinary noise had suddenly broken out on their left. It was shrill, it was harsh, and in fourteenth-century England it was undoubtedly unique.

'Brrrrrrrrrrrrrr,' it went, on and on and on, and it was soon joined by a rather muffled squealing and honking. Meg clutched Mr Stephen's arm and Jack stepped back but Edward, after one astonished moment, recognized the sound only too well. It had, in fact, woken him up many times in the past.

'Cripes!' he exclaimed. 'My alarm clock!'

And he took off over the grass and vanished down the dip in the land before anyone else realized what was happening. A strange sight met his eyes. Kneeling on the grass and with his head down on the ground, his arms round the back of his head as protection, was the small man in green. Beside him lay two heaving sacks from which the squealing and honking were coming, and in front of him was the Marks and Spencer carrier-bag with the contents all jumbled up on the grass and in the middle of them was the alarm clock flat on its face and ringing for all it was worth.

Edward slid down the bank and picked up the clock which stopped immediately.

'It's all right,' he said, forgetting in the excitement of the moment quite where he was. 'It only goes when it's face down you know and not always then. Actually it's never been the same since I dropped it. I suppose you hit it in some way and...'

'I never,' the little man said in a quavering voice, opening one eye, although he didn't lift his head from the ground, 'I never touched it. Honest.'

'You must have,' Edward replied, giving the clock a shake.

'Don't, don't,' the little man implored him, 'you'll start it off again as sure as eggs is eggs.'

'It won't hurt you,' said Edward and then added quickly, 'unless I tell it to that is. Why did you steal my things anyway?'

'Because I was hungry, that's why.'

He was, now Edward came to look at him properly, certainly very thin and his clothes were threadbare and extremely dirty. There was a pause during which three curious faces appeared over the top of the bank. Mr Stephen and Jack looked distinctly apprehensive, ut Meg, who had suddenly realized what the noise must have been, was having a hard time of it not to giggle.

'It's all right now,' said Edward, hastily pushing all his other belongings back into the bag. 'I've got rid of the noise. It's all gone.'

'So I hear,' said Mr Stephen, bravely climbing down the bank to join Edward. 'What was it?'

Edward thought of at least three replies, none of which would make any sense to a medieval Scavenger, and it was the small thief who unexpectedly came to his rescue by saying:

'It was a dreadful warning to me, that's what it was. I've never stole so much as a pig's ear before today and I never will again. No, not even if I was to starve to death, so there.'

'Oh no!' said Meg, joining them at the bottom of the bank, although Edward noticed that Jack, who was so brave about shooting the rapids, was still hanging back.

'Starve I shall,' the little man said simply. 'I'm pretty close to it now, I don't mind telling you. But work's hard to come by when you've got no trade. I'm one of a large family, see, and there wasn't enough land to support us all so I've had to fend for myself. An odd job here and a bit of work there is all I could hope for—not that I'm complaining mind. It's the way of the world. Well, I'm ready.' And he held up his wrists towards Mr Stephen who was frowning thoughtfully.

'Go on,' the little man said, 'I know the law. I stole this lad's valuables,' he shuddered at the memory, 'and two piglets *and* a goose. It's enough to hang me three times over, isn't it, governor?'

Mr Stephen nodded silently and Meg suddenly surprised even the startled Edward by snatching Tommy out of Mr Stephen's arms and saying wrathfully:

'I'll never speak to you again, never, never, NEVER if you hang him.'

'It won't be me that does the actual hanging,' said Mr Stephen.

'I don't care *who* does it,' said Meg, stamping her foot, 'you—you shan't do it. I'll tell my father, I will!' It was the worst threat she could think of and not a very good one as luckily only Edward realized.

'It *is* the law,' said Mr Stephen unhappily.

'Yes, but look here,' said Edward, 'supposing I won't say that he stole anything, wouldn't that make a difference?'

'Yes,' Mr Stephen admitted, 'but then there are the piglets and the goose you see.'

'But if we took them back to the Fair and let them loose nobody would ever know they'd *been* stolen,' said Edward. 'There are animals all over the place and...'

'Yes, they would,' interrupted Jack, who had now got up enough courage to look inside one of the sacks. 'This is Aunty's goose!'

There was something about his voice which made Edward, usually a boy who carefully avoided fights, long to hit him and apparently it had much the same effect on Jack's uncle for Mr Stephen suddenly said sharply:

'That's enough of that my lad and try and keep a civil tongue in your head. I know very well that you apprentices aren't above lifting an apple off a stall without paying for it if you get half a chance. And you've got no excuse at all because you're not starving and out of work, so shut up.'

'Please let him go,' pleaded Meg, trying to shush Tommy who had now woken up in a bad temper.

'I suppose I could,' Mr Stephen reflected, 'but it doesn't really solve the problem. Let's get the piglets back anyway, and the goose, and you – what is your name by the way?'

'Dick, please your honour,' said the thief who was still crouching on his knees with his wrists held up, an expression of faint hope on his thin face.

'You, Dick, come with us,' said Mr Stephen.

They managed to let the piglets out of the bag without anybody noticing. The animals appeared to be quite undistressed by their recent imprisonment and went scampering off towards the sow who was sitting in front of the cottages.

That was one problem out of the way!

'Aunty Mag!' called Mr Stephen.

The old woman hobbled out of the door leaning on a stick, her face puckered by distress.

'I've lost my Bessie,' she wailed. 'There was two of those dratted piglets came in here again and she went after them like the good goose she is and that's the last I've seen of her. I don't know what to do, I really don't. I've had Bessie from a gosling, and now she's gone and left me.'

'No she hasn't,' said Mr Stephen and he tipped up the sack and Bessie waddled out looking extremely bad-tempered, and with her feathers ruffled in fury. She pecked viciously at Dick's legs and scuttled into the dark security of her home.

'Well! Well I never did,' said Aunty Mag, sitting down with a thump on her stool.

'We found her,' Edward said quickly with a warning look at Jack—'at least Jack did.'

Jack went rather red and shifted his feet and then said in a low voice:

'We all did, it was Edward who found her first really.'

'Bless you,' said Aunty Mag, 'bless you both. I thought you had a lucky face, boy, the moment I saw you, even if you *are* a foreigner. Tell me where you live and the next time Bessie lays an egg I'll send it you as a treat.'

'Oh no, really,' Edward said, 'there's no need.'

'Go on,' Mr Stephen whispered, 'she wants to thank you and she hasn't much to give.'

'Well that'd be very kind of you,' said Edward. 'I'm Edward Hobson and I live at No. Six Farthing Row.'

He thought of adding the postal number and the date, too, for one wild moment.

'I'll remember that for you, Aunty,' said Mr Stephen airily. 'I can't say I know the place off-hand, but we'll find it. Now there is one other thing, Dick here.'

'I was wondering who he was,' said Aunty Mag who had been staring at the little man with her sharp old eyes in a way which made him feel very uneasy. 'He's a right bag of bones. A good meal wouldn't come amiss I shouldn't wonder.'

'He needs more than that,' said her nephew, 'what he really wants is a job. Look here, Dick, do you swear never to—er—you know what, again?'

'I swear it,' said Dick, 'and anyway I wouldn't dare, because of what he said,' and he nodded towards Edward. 'He's got magic powers he has. You can tell that just by looking at him.'

Everybody, even Meg, stared at the blushing Edward who to hide his embarrassment felt inside the paper carrier and brought out the packet of soup.

'Not really I haven't,' he mumbled, 'only where we come from they've got some jolly good ideas. This is one of them. You tear off this bit of paper—er—parchment—here and pour what's inside into boiling water, then you stir it up for a bit and it makes soup. I'd like you to have it for looking after the pram and everything.'

He handed the packet over to Aunty Mag who sniffed it suspiciously at first and then with growing pleasure.

'It certainly smells nice,' she agreed, 'thank you kindly. Will you stay for supper?'

'No thank you,' said Edward, 'we've got to be getting back—er—home. It's been great fun meeting you all.' They shook hands with everybody and Dick said hoarsely:

'I'll never forget what you've done, cross my heart and hope to die.'

'Yes, well,' said Edward, shuffling his feet and noticing in an absentminded way that even in fourteenth-century England his shoelaces had managed to come undone.

'What will you do with Dick?' Meg whispered to Mr Stephen.

'I'll give him work on my staff, we're always shorthanded. But if he so much as steals one *feather* from a goose I'll be down on him like a ton of cobbles. I hope we meet again, you're a nice pair, magic powers or not!' said Mr Stephen with a grin which plainly showed that he for one didn't believe they had any such thing.

'I hope we do too, and thank you ever so much,' said Meg and went on tiptoe to kiss his cheek, at which Mr Stephen frowned ferociously, for like many kind-hearted people he thoroughly disliked having his kindness noticed.

'Farewell,' said Jack, 'I'll teach you to skate if you ever come to London in the winter.'

'Thanks,' said Edward, 'and I'll teach *you* to read and write if you ever come to Farthing Row.'

'Which,' as he said to Meg as they pushed the pram away from the cottages, 'jolly well shut *him* up for a bit. He wasn't half as nice as Oofa.'

'No,' agreed Meg, 'but then Mr Stephen was far, far nicer than Oofa's father, so it works out about the same. At least they didn't put us in prison. Or Dick either. I do *hope* they like the soup.'

Owing to a slight miscalculation on Edward's part the spectacles took them back through time correctly enough, but landed them in space in the back garden of Number Four.

'It's all right,' said Edward, 'we're home. At least

nearly home. We must have walked further than I thought. It's jolly difficult to work out how far you've gone and I'll have to be more careful next time or we might land up anywhere. Gosh, I'm tired.'

As Meg was, too, they sat in the overgrown garden for a while and listened to the noise of the traffic and the sound of people talking and babies crying and children shouting.

'Except for the buses and cars it doesn't really sound so different from where we've been, does it?' Edward reflected sleepily. 'I quite liked it there. It's a pity in a way that we'll never meet any of them again.'

As it happened he was quite wrong for there was going to be a reunion, although under very different circumstances.

9. *The Third Journey*

'FANCY running into Old Mag,' said Miss Rose when Edward and Meg had told the two Miss Witchams about their last adventure, and the sisters had admired the rings which Meg had got by barter. 'She was a witch you know, quite a famous one in her time. I'd no idea she lived right here though, it's quite a coincidence. She was.'

'What?' Edward and Meg asked together.

'A white witch,' said Miss Lily, looking up from her latest batch of books from the library.

'They didn't do anything awful to her did they?' asked Meg anxiously.

'Because she was a witch you mean? Oh no, my dear. All that silly persecution business didn't start until hundreds of years later. Witches and wise women were highly respected before that. And I daresay Old Mag was even more honoured after the news of your packet soup got about,' said Miss Lily, chuckling.

'Well,' said Miss Rose briskly, 'we seem to be getting warmer, or rather you two do. At least some kind of laws were starting to operate on the Common.'

'You haven't heard the rest of the story,' said Edward, glancing at Meg. 'You see we had to get out of the garden of Number Four. We opened the back door all right and then it seemed rather a waste not to explore the house a bit.'

'It was ever so creepy,' said Meg, shivering slightly.

'Well it was a bit,' admitted Edward, 'because the windows were all covered up, so it was nearly dark inside. It's all dirty and dusty in there and there's some furniture up in the top room...'

'And mice in the kitchen,' put in Meg, shivering more than ever. 'I didn't want to stay, so I went and undid the front door and—' she took a deep breath—'that bossy man—you know...'

'Mr Chirk the Rehousing person?' suggested Miss Lily.

Meg nodded violently.

'He was going past and he saw me,' she said. 'He was awfully cross. He said it was trespass-something or other and that if we ever did it again there'd be Real Trouble.'

'He would,' said Miss Rose. 'He's a...'

'We weren't doing any harm either,' Edward put in in an injured voice. 'I tried to tell him, but he wouldn't listen. He just kept on the way he does. You know.'

'I do indeed,' agreed Miss Lily. 'He does it to us too, and your grandfather. He's one of those people who just listens to his own voice and nobody else's. He *made* us go and look at a flat on the Estate although we told him that nothing would ever get us to live there—any of us.'

'Never mind,' Miss Rose said brightly, 'third time lucky. You are prepared to have another?'

'Yes,' said Edward, 'but not tomorrow, because it's my turn to go and see a beastly flat.'

The Estate turned out to be several blocks of flats with courtyards separating them and a one-storey building to one side which, Mr Chirk informed the Commander with a bright smile, was the Club House.

'There'll be Bingo on Monday and Thursday nights,' he said. 'Old Folks' tea on a Wednesday, film shows on Tuesday, Young Folks' get-together on Fridays and a dance for teenagers on Saturdays.'

Edward and his grandfather exchanged appalled glances and even Jellicoe whined uneasily. Although it was another beautiful hot day the shadow of the flats seemed to fall across them coldly and then as they passed the playground, one of the boys who was climbing up the wire and pretending to be a monkey, which was dead easy for him as he looked like one to begin with, shouted out:

'Hallo Four-Eyes!'

'There,' said Mr Chirk, 'you see, Edward? You'll make friends in no time.'

The flat was small and very low down in the block,

for, as Mr Chirk pointed out, although they didn't expect old folk like the Commander to climb the stairs (since there was a perfectly good lift), it was just another little touch of foresight on the part of his department. So all they could see out of the windows was the wire round the playground, half the Club House, and a corner of the next door block.

'Nice, isn't it?' said Mr Chirk, apparently unaware of the three stony faces turned to his because even Jellicoe was looking sad. 'All mod cons as I said. Yes, we're very proud of our Estate, and we know folk are going to appreciate all the time and trouble we've taken on their behalf.'

There was a pause while he waited for somebody to say, 'Yes, rather,' or 'It's very nice', but there was only a long silence during which Grandfather thought of Number Six Farthing Row where he had lived all his long life and Edward thought of Mr Stephen and how, although he had lived six hundred years ago, he had somehow known that people wouldn't really want to live like this. Jellicoe wasn't thinking of anything, but his instinct was to get away from this place which had no nice familiar smells about it. So he pulled at his lead with his ears back, making a thin whining noise in the back of his throat.

'Off we go then,' said Mr Chirk. 'I've another lot to show round this afternoon you know. The family next door to you as it happens. We're putting them at the top of the furthest block as they're all – well – a little bit younger than you, Commander!' And he laughed heartily as he opened the door.

Even Jellicoe was silent on the walk back to the Row and it was Grandfather who spoke first as they crossed the road by the traffic lights with a train 'shushing' through the cutting behind them.

'There was a pond over there when I was a boy about your age,' he said, 'used to sail boats on it.'

'I know,' said Edward heavily. He still felt as though the shadow of the flats was looming up behind him and he wanted to get home. Not even the realization that where the 12 o'clock fast to Bournemouth was now roaring on its way, was the place where Dick the thief had tried to hide could make him feel more cheerful.

'I expect I've told you about it many times before,' said the Commander. 'To heel, Jellicoe!', and that was the end of the conversation – with no mention at all of the Estate, although it was in all their minds.

The Estate appeared to have had very much the same effect on Meg when she met Edward the following morning, for she wasn't at all her usual chirpy self and her underlip was pushed right out.

'He called me girlie,' she said, scowling.

'He called Grandfather an Old Folk,' replied Edward. 'Never mind, perhaps Miss Rose is right and it will be third time lucky. Let's go and get our orders.' But to their dismay, even Miss Rose seemed a little less bright than usual, although she did her best to hide it.

'My sister has been doing a great deal of homework,' she said, 'but the trouble is.'

'I can't find anything definite,' said Miss Lily, pushing her bent fingers through her white hair until it stuck up in small wisps. 'Thanks to you, Edward, and you too Meg, we know that the Common first became open land, so to speak, about 500 BC; and then it was certainly Common land in Edward the Second's time – not a very good king I'm afraid – with certain rules and regulations attached to it. As far as I can make out everything went on normally for another three hundred years and then there were sweeping changes and it all becomes rather blurred.'

'Couldn't we go there then?' asked Edward, doing some mental arithmetic. 'It must be when King Charles was—oh!'

'Exactly,' said Miss Rose earnestly, taking the fire-tongs away from Tommy who was sucking the polished knob on the handle. 'The Civil War.'

'What's a civil war?' asked Meg. 'I thought civil meant polite, you know like Mr Stephen saying "Can't you keep a civil tongue in your head?". Does it mean a polite war then?'

'It wasn't at all polite, it was extremely nasty,' said Miss Lily briskly. 'It was one half of England against the other. Neighbour fighting neighbour, brother killing brother.'

'I don't think I want to see any killing, thank you,' said Meg firmly.

'Nor me,' agreed Edward.

Miss Lily picked up her knitting and put it down again and Miss Rose went off to the kitchen and came back with an ivory ring which she gave to Tommy, saying:

'It's been boiled, so it's quite safe and there's no danger of.'

'Germs, thank you very much,' said Meg.

'The point is,' said Miss Lily, 'that I have come across a mention of a Sir Roger Farthing about that time. It's not much of a lead but it might mean something.'

Edward stared hard at the rocking-horse—in fact he looked clean through it and at the faded wallpaper beyond, for it was one of the pieces of furniture which always appeared to be misty when he was wearing his spectacles. He hated fighting and fighting where people actually got killed was even worse, but then he remembered the boy in the Estate playground and Grandfather being called an Old Folk. And after all he could always get away quickly if anything really bad happened, so he heaved a big sigh and picked up the school satchel which after having the Marks and Spencer bag stolen, seemed a safer bet.

'OK, I'll go,' he said.

'Splendid,' said Miss Lily quickly before he could change his mind. 'You're a brave boy, Edward.'

'I'm not really,' said Edward, going scarlet right up to the roots of his hair, for nobody had ever called him that before. In fact, as he never joined in the fights in the school playground, he was more used to being termed an 'old cowardy custard'. 'I don't like hitting people or being hit,' he added . . .

'But that's what I mean,' said Miss Lily. 'Any fool can start a fight; quite often courage doesn't come into it, just stupidity. Being brave is doing something when you don't want to do it but know you have to, because other people are depending on you. Now then . . .'

'I'll go too,' said Meg. 'I won't take Tommy because my mother wouldn't like him to be in a battle or anything, but if Edward can go then I can go.'

'You'd better not,' said Edward.

'Well I shall,' replied Meg, sticking out her underlip, and nothing anybody could say would make her change her mind, so Miss Lily quickly read a page in one of the library books and then outlined her plan for the adventurers.

'Well I don't suppose a few years are all *that* important; we'd better try for just after the war was over and see what happens. Here's your date, Edward,' and she pointed it out. 'We'll keep an eye on Tommy for you, Meg. I suppose you wouldn't care to start your journey here, Edward? I haven't seen any vanishing magic for more years than I care to remember...'

So in the middle of the parlour of Number One, Edward and Meg grasped hands; and not only a lot of the furniture, but the wall as well, grew misty and in a moment there was no sign of them at all.

'You should have told,' said Miss Rose severely.

'That there was still a lot of danger?' said Miss Lily. 'There was no point in meeting trouble halfway and, in any case, my faith in Edward's ability to deal with whatever may arise is growing all the time. There's a great deal of his grandfather in that boy. They'll be all right, you'll see. Now get my ball of wool away from that dratted kitten and stop fussing like a silly old woman!'

At the same moment Meg, her eyes still firmly shut, was saying:

'I can't hear any fighting.'

There was actually nothing to hear at all except the hoarse cry of a carrion crow. No people, no voices, no footsteps, no traffic. But there was a very nasty smell. Not the rich, strong smell of the Bronze Age forest, nor the spicy smell of the Medieval Fair, but a smell that was full of rottenness and decay.

Edward summed it up.

'It stinks,' he said. 'And there's nobody about so we're quite safe. Open up.'

They were standing in the centre of a small stone room with chipped marble slabs round the walls and rusted bars across the tiny broken window. The sky outside was dull and overcast and half hidden by ivy so that the room was dark, but not so dark that Meg couldn't see two green narrowed eyes watching her from the shadows.

'It's a rat,' she shrieked and she let go of Edward's hands and ran out of the door and down the passage before he could stop her. It was even darker out there and Edward had to follow the sound of her running footsteps because he couldn't see her at all.

'Come back, you idiot!' he shouted. 'Meg!'

He nearly tripped over a broken floorboard and narrowly avoided a gaping black hole, and when he touched the wall it felt wet and slimy. It was like running in a nightmare when what is in front may be even worse than what you are afraid of behind. Then there was a tremendous crash and the shrieking stopped and Edward felt himself go quite cold, but he kept up his stumbling run and in a moment he found himself enveloped in something soft and clinging and rather damp. He tore himself free his heart thundering, and then he gave a sob of relief as he realized that it was only an old curtain that had been hung across the doorway at the end of the long passage.

In front of him was a large hall with a wooden floor and with two broken staircases leading up to a kind of gallery. A lot of the roof was missing, so there was enough daylight to see by properly and in the middle of the floor was Meg on her hands and knees surrounded by broken pieces of armour.

'Are you all right?' demanded Edward, hauling her to her feet and almost shaking her in his anxiety.

'Oh! oh! oh!' was all Meg could say at first.

'I ran into that,' she went on, 'and it all came to pieces. And I'm not at all all right and I want to go home.'

'Well you can't. We've only just come.'

Edward picked up a piece of the armour and it was so rusted that it came in two in his hands. Apart from that and the curtain there didn't seem to be any other furniture at all. Some rings had been driven into one wall and a few bits of frayed rope hung down from them, so it looked as if the hall had once been used for tethering horses. Even the doors were missing from the doorways and, when Edward cautiously tiptoed over to look into one of the rooms, he saw that a great deal of the floor and the mantelpiece were gone too and all the panelling on the walls was splintered. It made him think of some of the houses which had been knocked down on one side of the Common, only somehow this place seemed even sadder, as though somebody had really enjoyed doing all the damage they could. He shivered and jumped as Meg said from right beside him:

'I don't like this place a bit. It's nasty.'

'It must have been a jolly big house once,' said Edward, turning round on his heel and looking up at where the roof had been. 'I wonder who lived here?'

A shadow stirred up in the long gallery and there was a soft creaking sound and then a man came into view. He was a big man whose clothes hung on him loosely. He had long, matted dark hair and there was a deep scar running down his face from his forehead to his chin. He had very bright eyes and there were patches of dull red on his cheeks, and he was breathing very fast as he looked down on the two figures below.

'I can tell you who lived here once,' he said in a hoarse whisper, 'Sir Roger Farthing, that's who,' and he began to laugh—a laugh that turned into a cough. He shook his head impatiently, braced himself and then, while Edward and Meg watched him in horrified fascination, he vaulted clean over the rotten balustrade and jumped to the floor below as lightly as a cat. In six rapid strides he reached Edward and gripped him by the shoulder.

'Sir Roger Farthing,' he repeated, 'that's what you wanted to know, wasn't it, you rotten little spy?' And his grip tightened.

10. *The Highwayman*

'I'M NOT a spy,' said Edward, bristling, just as he had done when old Mag had called him a foreigner. 'I only wanted to know because I was interested, that's all, and if it's your house I'm sorry.'

The man looked at him with surprise and laughed and coughed again.

'Me—Sir Roger?—what a jest!' he said. 'If you're not spies who are you?'

'Travellers,' said Edward.

'Visitors,' said Meg, from behind him. Now that she could see the man more closely she wasn't quite so frightened of him, because, although he had an angry look, she had a feeling that it wasn't Edward and herself that he was angry with. His leap seemed to have exhausted him because he let go of Edward and went over to sit on the bottom stair, wiping his forehead with a tattered scarf.

'Most people avoid this place like the plague,' he said. 'They think it's haunted and so it is—by me.' And he laughed again, only sadly this time.

'Why do you haunt it?' Edward asked.

'Memories,' the man said slowly. 'I lived here once, not *in* the house, but round the back. I was a stable lad. Ah, we had some lovely horses then...' His voice dwindled into silence.

'Go on,' Edward said encouragingly.

'What's the good of remembering?' the man said sharply. 'What's past is past and best forgotten. Those days won't come back. Now begone. This is no place for children—Now—', and with surprising swiftness he drew an enormous pistol out from under the skirt of his shabby coat and pointed it at them. 'Don't *you* go remembering either. You never saw me, right?'

'Why not?' asked Edward, his curiosity getting the better of his fear of the blunderbuss.

'Questions, questions, because I say so, that's why! What does it matter anyway—I'm as good as dead. Perhaps that's why I came back here, I know not...' He seemed to be speaking to himself rather than to Edward and Meg, and he didn't even lift his head to watch them leave, but went on muttering under his breath.

The Common had changed a great deal since their last visit. There was no sign of the cottages, naturally, as their place had been taken by the big, sprawling house —or what remained of it. Most of the trees had gone from the north side too, and they could see the grey glint of the Thames with a few boats on it. London seemed to have spread quite a lot and there was a pall of smoke hanging over the course of the river. The road had grown wider, but the surface was very pitted and rough and now, as it started to rain softly and puddles formed, it was obvious that it would soon become extremely muddy. Straggly bushes grew quite close to the roadside and there was one big oak tree which creaked gently in the slight breeze. Something hung down from one of the branches and Edward, after one horrified glance, hastily turned the other way and pointed vaguely at the river valley.

'Not many houses are there?' he asked, trying to ignore the rattling noise which came from the tree.

'Not between us and London there aren't,' agreed Meg, who was still thinking about the man they'd just met. 'What do you think was the matter with him?'

'I don't know,' Edward replied shortly.

The Common was getting him down, it was so silent and empty. At least on the last two occasions they'd visited it there'd been other people about and a feeling that something, even if it was only an argument about a lost ox, was going on. But now there was nothing and it was as if the whole place was dead. He didn't like it one little bit.

'I think he's ill,' said Meg. 'My Dad had flu last winter and he looked just like that, all funny round his eyes.'

'We've drawn a real blank this time,' muttered Edward, hitching his satchel more comfortably round his shoulders. 'There's nobody to ask about the Common,' and he kicked at the long unkempt grass.

'There's him,' said Meg, nodding towards the house.

'He told us to be gone. He drove us away.'

'We'd better go home then, it's no good just standing here getting wet,' Meg said practically. It was obviously the sensible thing to do, but it seemed a rather tame ending to the voyage and Miss Lily had said that Sir Roger might be a possible lead, so after a moment's further thought Edward shrugged and said:

'Perhaps he might tell us something. It's worth a try anyway.'

'Supposing he shoots us?' said Meg, hanging back.

'Oh, it takes ages to load and use those old guns,' said Edward, hoping that what he was saying was true. 'We'd be back in Farthing Row before he could do it. Come on.'

The man was still sitting where they had left him, his hands hanging loosely between his knees.

'I thought I told you to be off,' he growled.

'There was nowhere to be off to,' Edward replied, 'and it was starting to rain.'

It was raining indoors as well as outside because of the broken roof, and small puddles were already forming on the rotting floor. The man looked at them steadily for a moment and then shrugged in much the same way as Edward had done.

'Fugitives like me, eh?' he said. 'Only all you're hiding from is a wetting, while as for me,' and he drew his hand across his throat. 'Come into my parlour then, only mind the stairs, most of 'em have either rotted away or been eaten by rats. Give me your hand, girl.'

His hand was hot and dry in hers and she could feel him shaking a little as they slowly climbed the staircase and he led them into a room which was blacked out with dark stuff nailed over the windows.

'I've got a candle here somewhere,' he muttered, and jumped with fright as Edward lit a match. 'That was quick work,' he said admiringly, and he picked up a candle and held it out for Edward to light. The flame flickered and shadows jumped up and down on the walls, but they could see that there was a heap of bedding against one and a very battered oak bench. The room smelt musty and damp, but it wasn't as bad as it had been downstairs.

'I'd offer you some food if I had any,' the man said, sinking down on to the bedding', 'but you've caught me at a bad time. Last month, now, things were very different. Strange what things happen.'

'Food?' said Edward, sliding the satchel off his back and opening it. 'I've got some food if you'd like a bite.'

'I won't refuse,' the man replied, his eyes fixed on the satchel and glittering more than ever in the candlelight. Edward produced a tin of spaghetti in tomato sauce, and a tin opener, and then he realized that in spite of all his careful planning he'd forgotten a spoon. The man didn't mind at all though, for the moment the tin was opened he pulled it out of Edward's hands, sniffed it and then shut his eyes and began to tip the spaghetti into his mouth. It is messy enough stuff at the best of times and eaten in this way it was even messier, but the man didn't care and in thirty seconds flat the tin was empty and he was running one finger round the inside and then sucking it.

Edward watched this performance with his own mouth wide open, and silently passed over a bar of chocolate which vanished in rapid silence.

'Strange food, but palatable,' the man said, wiping his cuff across his mouth, 'I suppose you haven't any ale...?'

Edward got out the bottle of fizzy lemon and, although it made the man screw up his face, he swallowed it to the last drop and then hiccuped loudly.

'Pardon,' he said and then, for the first time since they'd met him, he smiled as though he meant it. 'That was good of you,' he said, 'but I suppose you realize you're assisting a fugitive from justice? There's nothing I can do for you in return for your kindness, except get you hanged like me!'

'Everybody's always getting hanged in history,' said Meg, who was sitting with her feet up on the bench just in case there were any rats up here too.

'Quite a lot of people were—and are,' the man agreed, 'or else it's the block. I'd prefer that myself because with hanging they cut you down before you're a goner and then...'

'I know,' said Edward, who had suddenly remembered about drawing and quartering and didn't want to hear the details at first hand. Somehow it was different from reading about it in history. 'There is something you could do for us though, tell us about Sir Roger Farthing.'

'I thought you said you weren't spies,' the man said, his hand going to his gun.

'We're not, cross my heart and spit on the ceiling, only we want to find him,' Edward said hastily.

'Then you'll have a long journey, young master. He's over the water in the Low Countries. Same as I should be if I had any sense. Same as I was once, come to that.'

'Go on, please,' urged Meg, 'we won't tell on you, Mr—er?'

'You can call me Ben, it's as good a name as any other

and what you don't know won't hurt you. My father was in service with Sir Roger and his father before that, and his father before *that*, so natural enough I came to work for him too. He was Lord of the Manor in those days—before the pair of you were born.'

Edward and Meg exchanged glances but wisely held their tongues.

'This was a lordly place then, though you might find it hard to think so now. I daresay there were as many as twenty indoor servants and as many more outside. We worked hard, mind, old Sir Roger was a real tartar, sailed against that Spanish lot of brigands he did, but he was fair with it. If you did a job well he'd thank you for it and then when he died, young Sir Roger he took over and he was just like his papa, in spite of he wore a lace collar and curled his hair. He might have looked a bit soft, but he wasn't underneath...' and Ben smiled, fingering the scar on his cheek.

'He didn't do that to you, did he?' Meg asked.

'Nah!' Ben laughed and then coughed, catching his breath. 'I got that at Worcester. But I'm jumping ahead a bit. Sir Roger he had a town house, right in London it was. He took me there a couple of times and a real fine place it seemed to me, but it wasn't home like here. Anyway, all this trouble started between the King and his Parliament, I didn't understand the half of it, but we all had to take sides and Sir Roger he was a King's man, so natural I was too. All of us out here in the country were, but some of those town servants they didn't have no sense of loyalty, they followed Old Noll.' And he spat suddenly on the floor.

'Old?' said Meg, looking enquiringly at Edward.

'Cromwell.'

'That's right, Old Noll we called him. A lot of the city stuck to his side, they knew which side their bread was buttered. Well, first off it looked as if we were going to win hands down, but the money began to run out, see. Sir Roger he melted down all his silver to help and so did a lot of other people, but it wasn't enough. The King he was defeated and taken prisoner and in the end...' He made the familiar sign across his throat. 'Off with his head. It was a shock I can tell you. Only a little fellow he was, but he was the King just the same and they shouldn't ought to have done it. I've heard tell he took it bravely.'

'He did,' said Edward warmly.

'Ah,' Ben sighed, 'well then his son, young Charles, he was crowned King up in Scotland and he came down south after a bit and we had this battle at Worcester. I wasn't supposed to fight, of course, being only there to look after my master's horses, but I couldn't just stand by so I took a sword off a chap that was dead—after all he wouldn't need it no more—and in I went. I didn't know nothing about real fighting, but I had a go and Sir Roger he saw me. He didn't half laugh although he had Old Noll's lot all round him, and yelling and cursing fit to bust he was. No, he wasn't soft.'

'And then?' Edward prompted as Ben fell silent.

'We lost again. We shouldn't have done, but we did. I saw King Charles come past, he'd have gone on with the battle to my way of thinking, but they was all telling him to get away, and...'

'What was he like?' Edward couldn't help asking.

'Like? Well, he was only a lad and dead ugly at that with a face as brown as a gipsy's. He was tall too, as far as I could judge, seeing as how he was on horseback. Anyway, next thing I knew we were off across country as hard as we could go. Sir Roger he was all for sending me back here, but I wouldn't have it so we went to France. I'd never been to sea before, never even seen it.

It was horrible,' he shuddered, 'and I didn't like it when we got to the other side neither. They called me a foreigner. Me!'

Edward laughed and Ben, after looking at him suspiciously for a moment, joined in.

'Well it's not nice, is it?' he said. 'All over Europe we went. I daresay it's all right if you're used to that kind of thing, but I got homesick after a bit, and Sir Roger he quite understood. He felt the same to my way of thinking. Anyway there was a price on his head, see, but there wasn't none on mine. So he arranges for me to get a boat from the Low Lands—a nasty wet place that was too—and back I came. But it wasn't the same. Everything had changed and all the people were going about with faces as long as today and tomorrow and you couldn't get no work unless you'd got references, which of course I hadn't so...'

'So?' queried Edward.

'So I took to the road.'

'You mean you became a tramp,' said Meg.

'Tramp! Never!' replied Ben, drawing himself up majestically and then rather spoiling the effect by coughing. 'I became a Gentleman of the Road, a Highwayman, see?'

'Oh,' said Edward, 'yes, I do see. Were you successful?'

'I was quite the gentleman,' Ben said, grinning. 'Money for old rope it was (not that I like the expression). There's a lot of people who were making good money in the City and trying to stash it away without anybody knowing. I soon caught on as to what was happening, and seeing as how I know this Common like the back of my hand, I come back here and night after night I'd hide in the bushes and wait for the sound of the coach wheels. Yes, I done very well for myself and somehow it didn't seem like stealing when you took the stuff off them lot. I don't say that my poor old father isn't turning in his grave at what I'm doing, but then he never knew how things'd be. So I tucked myself away here although it made me feel a bit rough when I saw what they'd done to the place. Quartered their horses here in the hall they had, and taken away all the furniture and that. The damage was something fierce, but it was Home just the same.'

He had another fit of coughing, which was so bad that Meg got off the bench and thumped him on the back.

'Thanks,' Ben said hoarsely. 'Anyway about a month ago I stopped a fat, important party and relieved him of his valuables. I was quite enjoying myself when a squad of soldiers suddenly loomed out of the darkness and started shooting. Of course I had to make a run for it and...' he hesitated. 'Well, the long and short of it was that I lamed my poor old Beauty getting away. I've put a poultice on her, but her fetlock's still up like a bowl of porridge and I can't leave her, so here I am stuck. And now they're out looking for me and me with a price on my head good and proper by this time. It's been a long ride, but I reckon this is the end of it, see. A man can run so far, but no further. I've come back to where I belong and...'

He stopped and held his breath and so did Edward and Meg as apart from the steady drip-drip-drip of the rain they heard something else, the clop of horses' hooves and the jingle of armour and the creak of leather.

In one bound Ben was off his seat and had his hand over Edward's mouth.

'I thought you said you weren't no spy,' he hissed, his grip tightening.

11. *Dick-the-Soldier*

'HE's not, he's not,' Meg cried frantically as she grabbed at Ben's arm. 'Oh please let him go, please!'

Slowly Ben's grip loosened and Edward, who had been almost suffocated, took several deep breaths. He and Meg could of course escape within a few seconds, but Ben's story had made a great impression on Edward, and instead of being angry at being accused of being a spy he only said huskily:

'Shut up both of you and let me think.'

The sound of the horsemen grew nearer, but something about the way Edward had spoken made both Ben and Meg keep quiet. Miss Lily Witcham had been quite right, Edward had changed a great deal lately.

'Let me go and talk to them,' said Edward. 'They can't touch me, I'll be quite safe. Meg, you'd better come too. Ben, stay here.'

'But—' said Ben, reaching for his pistol.

'No,' interrupted Edward, 'we didn't warn anybody, no matter what you may think, and I don't see why they *should* catch you. Come on, Meg,' and he took hold of her hand and pulled her out of the room just as a voice down below called out the commands:

'Halt! Dismount!'

There was a great deal more jingling and creaking, and a murmur of voices, and as Edward still holding tightly to Meg's wrist, carefully descended the staircase, a small man wearing a leather coat and breeches and an armour breastplate stalked into the hall holding aloft a burning torch. He stopped short when he saw the two on the stairs and said in a surprised voice:

' 'Pon my honour, two brats!'

'That's right,' Edward agreed cheerfully. 'Who did you think it was?'

'That's enough, boy,' replied the soldier. 'We're after a dangerous criminal, that's what, and if you know anything...' he added in a threatening tone, and as he raised the flaming torch Edward saw the man's face clearly under the steel helmet and his eyes widened in surprise.

'Why, you're Dick!' he exclaimed.

'Dick's my name for sure,' the soldier agreed, 'though how *you* should...wait a moment. Your face is familiar.'

'I'm Edward and this is Meg. Surely you remember! We met at—' and then he stopped, for the Dick he knew had lived some three hundred and fifty years before, and although he resembled the small wiry man who now stood in the hall below, he could not, of course, be the same person. All the same, the soldier was looking extremely puzzled.

'Hold hard,' he said, frowning, 'I do seem to recall that we might have met—once, but for the life of me I can't think where or when.'

'It was a long time ago,' gabbled Edward, 'and you owe me a good turn, honestly you do.'

The soldier shook his head and then grinned.

'Can't have been all that long ago,' he said, 'or you wouldn't have been born, m'lad. All the same there *is* something at the back of my mind. Wait there a moment.'

He stamped off to what had once been the front door and shouted some orders while Meg whispered fiercely. 'What are we going to do! We'll be hanged, too!'

'Well, you don't want Ben to be caught do you? Or do you?' said Edward.

'No, not really, but...' and then Dick came clumping back and Meg held her tongue. He had put on a bit of weight and was much more sure of himself, but it was the same face, there was no doubt about that.

'Now then,' he said, stripping off his gauntlet gloves, 'what's all this? Why are the two of you hiding out here, eh? This is no place for children. We're after a wanted man.' And even as he spoke came the clop-clop of more horses and an all too familiar voice drawled:

'I'm of some consequence I'll have you know and I

haven't got all day to dally here. I've plenty to do in the City.'

Edward, the soldier and Meg exchanged glances and suddenly they didn't seem to be on opposite sides at all as Edward recognized the speaker.

'It's the Headman *again*,' he exclaimed.

And Meg whispered:

'Why, it's Mr Chirk!'

And the soldier said hoarsely:

'It's the magistrate as was robbed last month.'

Something about the way he said it made Edward realize that perhaps there might be a way out of this after all.

'Come with us,' he said, and he took the soldier by the wrist and pulled him up the rotting staircase and into the room where Ben was standing with his blunderbuss levelled at the doorway.

'Put it down, do,' Edward began and then stopped as he saw Ben lower the pistol with a jerk and the soldier nearly drop his flaming torch.

'Stap me,' growled Ben in a hoarse voice, 'if it isn't—'

'I know you,' replied the soldier, 'you were with Sir Roger...'

'And I know *you*,' Ben broke in, 'one of his town servants *you* was. So it's come to this has it, one side of the house of Farthing against the other, that's a nice state of affairs I must say.'

'You mean you know each other?' asked Meg.

'Know each other? That's a good 'un,' Ben said, coughing painfully. 'Ask him if he wasn't in Sir Roger's service as a—a...'

'Footman,' the soldier said. 'Yes I was, and not ashamed of it neither. I come from a good City family I do, and all good Cromwell men we are too. All the same...'

There was a long silence while they looked at each other, and Edward remembered Miss Lily's words about brother killing brother, and dimly he understood what she had meant about the war being so terrible because, although these two men facing each other in the flickering candlelight were not related, they had once been friends. He decided to take a chance and said quickly:

'Dick, that is, sir, you won't give him up, will you? Remember how once upon a time you were nearly hung and...'

'Nearly hanged! Me!' cried the soldier. Frowning, he looked at Edward and Meg, muttering as he shook his head. 'It's strange you should say that. I have had dreams, betimes. But that cannot be...All the same I have no wish to see a fellow servant of former days go to the gallows. There's been enough hangings already to my way of thinking. Nevertheless, duty is duty and he *is* a highwayman.'

'Fair enough,' Ben agreed, 'I am that and nobody can escape the gallows for ever. I'm sick and tired of running and that's the truth. I come back here thinking I'd find my home again, but it's gone for ever. I liked working for Sir Roger and I loved my horses, but...', and he shrugged his shoulders and coughed.

'You can't do this,' Edward said fiercely to the soldier. 'He's down on his luck just like you were in—that is lots of people have...' He stopped as he thought of the Miss Witchams and Meg's family and Grandfather and Jellicoe. A shadow hung over them, too—in a kind of a way—and, although it wasn't as bad as being hanged, it was a shadow that encompassed them too.

The soldier swung backwards and forwards on his heels, looking first at Ben and then at Edward and

Meg, his brow furrowed as though he was trying to work something out. At last he said abruptly:

'I don't want to arrest Ben. I'm sick and tired of all this business too and that's a fact. But what can I do? The law's the law – funny I remember somebody saying that a long time ago – so I've not got much choice.'

'Supposing he vanishes,' Edward said. 'Vanishes for ever and ever, would that do?'

'Vanishing isn't that easy,' the soldier replied, 'not when the place is surrounded. All the same if there was a way – and him and me were friends once – well, I wouldn't be one to stand in your path.'

'OK,' Edward said, taking a deep breath, 'we'll take him with us if you don't...'

'How?' said Meg. 'You don't mean –'

'What about my horse, Beauty?' Ben asked.

'I'll look after her,' the soldier said, his eyes on Edward. 'I do remember now. We have met before, a long, long time ago although I don't exactly recall when.'

'I do,' Edward said. 'And thanks, thank you very much. Ben take my hand and you too, Meg.'

'You can't...' Meg protested.

'It's the only thing to do,' Edward replied. 'Come on quick, before the soldiers and you-know-who get back.'

Even as he spoke there was the noise of clanking armour and creaking leather and a very important-sounding voice saying:

'I tell you fellows I am a *very* responsible person with a great deal of influence...'

'Hurry, hurry,' Edward said, grasping the hot, dry hand of Ben, and then as their footsteps pounded up the broken staircase, and a round familiar figure appeared in the doorway he wished, and as everything began to dissolve in the swirling mist, Edward spoke directly to the soldier who was standing stolidly beside the flickering candle.

'You'll be all right!' he shouted.

And as the clouds thickened Dick yelled back.

'It's witchcraft! Come back, come back I say!' but he managed a wink as he spoke, his face masked with an expression of utter astonishment.

As the travellers had arrived in one of the larders at Farthing Manor, and started their journey back in a bedroom, when the mist cleared and Edward was able to get his bearings he thought for one dreadful moment that they hadn't got away at all. They were in semi-darkness in the middle of a dilapidated room with a faint musty smell about it. At length with a sigh of thankfulness he recognized his surroundings.

'We're in the top bedroom of Number Four,' he said.

'Thank goodness,' said Meg, 'oh I *am* glad to be back.'

Ben opened his eyes too and then shut them again, muttering huskily to himself.

'It's the fever,' he said. 'I've never felt this bad before, not even on that fishing boat. Where's Dick the footman gone?'

'He's gone a long, long way away,' Edward said comfortingly. 'You're quite safe now,' and he pushed the trembling highwayman into a sagging old armchair which stood by the window, and took Meg to one side and whispered:

'We'll have to keep him here for a bit. I think you're right and he has got flu which is a stroke of luck in a way. You know how everything seems funny and odd when you've got a temperature.'

'Suppose Mr Chirk comes back?' Meg enquired.

'We'll just have to keep our fingers crossed that he won't. Shh, Ben's going to sleep.'

They studied him doubtfully. He certainly did look quite ill, and Meg who knew just how to look after Tommy when he was off colour, put a box under Ben's feet in their tattered boots, and wrapped his coat more tightly round him, then she tiptoed down the dusty stairs after Edward. They managed to slip out of the house without anybody seeing them, and they raced down the path to Number One where Miss Lily had just started on the second row of her knitting.

'A highwayman! Just fancy!' Miss Rose said admiringly as the story was poured out. 'I've always heard that there were one or two of them out this way, it's one of the main roads to the coast you see. Poor man, what's to become of him?'

'Exactly,' said Miss Lily. 'You were quite right to rescue him, Edward, but we must consider his future.'

'I suppose,' Edward said slowly, 'you couldn't...?'

Miss Lily put down her knitting and rubbed the side of her nose with one needle while everybody looked at her hopefully.

'There are all the *forms*,' she said. 'Birth certificate, national insurance card, a doctor's card...this is the age of documents. He could never get any kind of work without them. He might even drift back into a life of crime again, which would be a dreadful thing. I'm not saying that I couldn't have a try at—er—dealing with the situation, but it's so easy to make a mistake with modern equipment. Remember the gas-meter, Rose?'

'Yes,' Miss Rose nodded, 'that gas-man *was* astonished. Still there's no need to worry about all that just yet. The first thing is to see that he gets rid of that nasty cough. I've got just the plant growing in the garden and I'll go and.' She left the room only to put her head round the door again to mutter, 'Blankets and a bottle too,' and was gone.

'At least we have made a step forward,' said Miss Lily. 'You say there was only one house on the Common, Edward? Now that's most interesting, for it shows that there was a great deal more open land a mere three hundred or so years ago. I rather feel we may be on to something. One further point, you must let us pay for the spaghetti, and chocolate, and any other little expenses you may have had. No, no, I insist. It will be our part of the business as, after all, the pair of you are doing all the hard work. Meg dear, I think Tommy is trying to eat my ball of wool.'

It soon became obvious that looking after the highwayman was going to be quite a problem as far as getting in and out of Number Four was concerned.

'I don't see how anybody can choose to be a burglar, it's too scaring,' said Edward when he and Meg had experienced their third narrow escape in two days. Once they had been nearly spotted by the milkman, the second time it was a very puzzled looking postman with a large parcel, and on the third occasion they nearly walked slap into the Commander who was out walking Jellicoe.

'Ah there you are,' he said, apparently unaware that Edward and Meg, both rather white-faced, were coming out of the wrong house. 'Been wondering where you'd got to, boy. There's another of those dratted officials coming round to see me this afternoon. You'd better be there too and you as well if you like Peg.'

'Meg,' said Meg.

'Meg, Peg, all the same thing. And while you're at it, better ask your parents along and the Miss Witchams. Perhaps if we all get together...'

'My parents are out at work,' Meg replied stiffly, 'but they've both been down to the Town Hall in their dinner-times. They said it didn't do any good.'

'One last final try,' the Commander said. 'I'll go and call on the ladies at Number One and then I'll make a cake.'

'Can he?' whispered Meg.

'He's jolly good at it,' Edward replied. 'He's trying to teach me, but I keep on dropping the eggs. I hope it's not old Headman Chirk.'

But it wasn't, for when the man from the Council arrived he turned out to be quite tall with a thin, rather worried face, very bright blue eyes and grey hair, and when Meg who had been hovering anxiously by the front door opened it for him and he smiled she knew him at once.

'Why, you're Stephen the Scavenger and you've shaved off your beard!' she said in amazement.

The man stepped back a pace looking equally astonished.

'Well no,' he said with a twinkle, 'I'm afraid not. I'm only Mr Stephen Scaiffe, the Borough Surveyor, and I've never had a beard. But may I come in just the same?'

12. *The Fourth Journey*

'IT'S MOST odd you know,' said Mr Scaiffe to Miss Lily Witcham between mouthfuls of the Commander's excellent lemon sponge, 'but that little girl greeted me as Stephen the Scavenger. Odd, because I believe that hundreds of years ago one of my forebears was a member of that profession. They were what you might call the Borough Surveyors of their day.'

'Very odd,' agreed Miss Lily, 'but then I've often thought that young people see things that we don't,' and she gave a little chuckle.

'Order, order,' said the Commander, knocking on the table with a teaspoon. 'We've all come here today, Mr Scaiffe, to try to make you change your mind. Isn't there any way of saving the Row?'

'None that I can find,' Mr Scaiffe replied sadly. 'I'm very fond of this little row of houses myself, I've known them all my life. In fact, Commander Hobson, a long time ago I was one of those boys who used to climb over your wall to try and steal an apple or two. I always wanted to live here myself.'

'Did I ever catch you?' the Commander asked with interest.

'Once. You gave me the telling-off of my young life, I've never forgotten it. But to get back to the Row, we haven't got many old period houses in our Borough, goodness knows, and I did have a shot at saving them on those grounds. Unfortunately it didn't work. The extra common land has got to be found somewhere you see, and this is the obvious choice. I'm very sorry.'

There was a short silence, which was broken only by Tommy sucking noisily on a sugar lump.

'Lived here all my life,' the Commander said, 'as these two ladies have. It's what we're used to. These houses are part of us. Take us away and put us in some beastly modern Estate and it's like chopping off our roots.'

'Agreed,' said Miss Lily.

'Very well put. I couldn't have put it better myself not even,' said Miss Rose, nodding, and then she added, 'If only we had a little more time,' and she glanced at

Edward and then Meg, who was trying to slide a piece of cake into a paper bag on her lap as she thought the highwayman might fancy a slice now he was starting to feel a little better.

'No place in this modern world for us old people,' the Commander said fiercely. 'The next thing we know we'll be being bundled off into some institution with nothing to do and...'

'Wait,' Mr Scaiffe interrupted. 'Now then, let me think,' and he clasped his hands together, quite forgetting he was still holding some cake. He wiped his fingers in an absentminded way, scowling with concentration. 'I wonder...' he said slowly, 'it's worth a try...I wonder if I could put up a plan to have the three empty houses in the middle of the row converted into one!'

'Don't see what good that would do,' barked the Commander, whose hopes had shot upwards for one dizzy moment only to come crashing down again.

'You don't understand,' said Mr Scaiffe. 'I mean converted into a properly run home for elderly people. We're desperately short of accommodation in the Borough and it might, it just might work—although there's still the problem of finding the extra common land. Look here, I'll drive back to the Town Hall immediately and get out the old plans of this row and see if anything *can* be done. It's a bit of a forlorn hope, but anything's better than nothing.'

It was, as he said, a very small chance, but at least, as Edward said while he and Meg were doing the washing-up, it was worth a try.

'And to think that we were taken prisoner by the Headman and had all your things stolen and we nearly got caught by Roundheads, all for nothing,' said Meg.

'Well you got that bronze bracelet and the rings and

we did save Dick from getting hung, and we did rescue Ben, as well as getting Oofa out of trouble,' Edward reminded her. 'And you'd better take Ben his cake before it all goes into crumbs.'

Meg had borrowed her father's razor and the highwayman had just finished using it as they crept up the stairs. He looked a great deal better and his cough had nearly gone, but he was starting to get restless.

'It's not that I'm not grateful, I am,' he said. 'You've saved my life and I won't never forget it, but I'm an open-air man myself and I want to get out and stretch my legs. I don't know what country this is you've brought me to, nor how we got here neither, but I'd like to have a look at it. Funny sort of place it seems to be with all these lights and noises. I never heard such a noise as you've got here. Worse than the Battle of Worcester it is. No offence meant and none taken I hope?'

'Granted,' said Edward gallantly. 'It's—it's a bit difficult at the moment, so if you could hang on another day or two...'

Apart from the difficulty of keeping Ben hidden it was getting to be quite an expensive business too, now that his appetite was improving; and then suddenly a new and far worse danger loomed up without warning, just twenty-four hours after the tea-party. Meg was trying rather inexpertly to darn an enormous hole in the highwayman's stocking, while Tommy crawled round the floor looking for things to bite on, and Ben was showing Edward how his pistol worked, when there was the sound of voices down below. Everybody was quiet except Tommy who said:

'Ed, Ed, Ed.'

'That's odd,' said a voice from the hall, 'I thought I heard someone.' It was Mr Scaiffe who, knowing how desperately little time was left before the Row was to be demolished, had been as good as his word and started the campaign to turn Numbers Four, Three and Two into a home for elderly people.

'Nonsense, place is empty. Been empty over a year,' said the voice of Mr Chirk impatiently. 'Smells like it too. If you ask me, Scaiffe, your plan hasn't a hope of succeeding, far better to knock the whole row down and be done with it.'

'Just let's have a look round, now we're here,' Mr Scaiffe said firmly. 'Ah, here come my assistants. There's no harm in measuring the houses up after all.'

'I'm a very busy man,' Mr Chirk said, 'and this hare-brained scheme of yours...' His voice died to a murmur as two more men came into the hall and they all began to talk at once.

'What are we going to do?' breathed Meg, snatching up Tommy as though to protect him.

'Are they your enemies?' whispered Ben, grasping his pistol more firmly.

'Hide,' said Edward. But there wasn't anywhere *to* hide, and they hadn't a chance of getting down the stairs unnoticed.

'One of them's our friend and one is our enemy and I don't know about the other two,' replied Meg, desperately trying to stop Tommy from calling out by putting him against her shoulder and rubbing his back.

The murmur of voices grew louder and then to their horror they heard Mr Scaiffe say.

'I'll start at the top. Want to come and look, Chirk?'

'Oh very well, but I haven't got all day...'

There were footsteps on the dusty stairs, one lot light and quick and the other heavy and slow.

'Quick, quick,' said Edward. 'Hold hands and shut your eyes.'

'I can't,' Meg said desperately, 'I've got Tommy.'

'Sit down and put him on your lap then, only hurry!'

They all scrambled down on to the floor, but they were too late for the door had already been opened and Mr Scaiffe was inside the room before he realized anybody else was there. He stared at them, his eyes going round as buttons and his jaw sagging.

'What—what—what...' he said.

'Just coming,' wheezed Mr Chirk. 'Caught a couple of kids in here not long ago, did I tell you? If I ever lay my hands on them again...'

It was no time to hesitate. Edward came to a rapid decision, seized one of the Borough Surveyor's hands and pulled him into the circle, snapping at Ben.

'He's our friend. Take his other hand. Everybody SHUT YOUR EYES!'

He said this so firmly that everybody obeyed without question, even Mr Scaiffe, although he was still saying faintly 'What? What? What?' as the coloured clouds closed round them and all the wishing instructions that Edward could think of were:

'Sanctuary...'

'What on earth *is* going on?' wailed Mr Scaiffe faintly. If finding Edward, Meg and Tommy in the house had not been enough, discovering a man in shabby seventeenth-century clothes with a blunderbuss in his hand was sufficient to unsettle anybody.

'We're there,' said Edward.

'Where?' asked Meg.

'*I* don't know,' Edward replied, getting his breath back.

'What *is* going on?' repeated Mr Scaiffe plaintively.

'Don't ask me, sir,' said Ben, shaking his head. 'I thought I was over the fever, but it's come back worse than ever now.'

They were standing in the top room of Number Three. It was the same yet somehow different. The floor was brand new, so new that it was still covered in wood shavings. The window had shrunk a little and had no glass in it and the roof above their heads was only half finished. The smell was the most pleasant that they had yet come across, with the scent of wood and flowers and new-mown grass all mixed up together.

Edward went over to the window and looked out. He saw several men grouped round a horseman who was leaning down to listen to what they were saying. He was wearing a tightly buttoned coat, with long tails, very close fitting trousers and long boots. He had a square, pleasant face and, as though aware that he was being watched, he glanced up and shouted:

'Hi, you up there? What do you think you're doing, eh?'

He sounded amused rather than annoyed, and Edward was just about to try and think of an answer when he found himself being picked up as though he weighed nothing at all and pushed to one side.

'Sir Roger!' Ben muttered hoarsely. 'It's my master, it is, it is...'

He gripped the edge of the window-sill, staring down at the horseman, his face so white that the scar stood out lividly.

Meg and Edward exchanged extremely puzzled glances, for how could it possibly be Sir Roger Farthing on the Common when he was living in exile in the Low Countries? But that point didn't seem to worry Ben. With a sudden excited snort of laughter he dashed past them and down the stairs.

'Would somebody,' pleaded Mr Scaiffe in a low voice, '*please* tell me what's happening?'

'We don't know,' Edward replied, 'honestly we don't. Please don't worry anyway, you're quite safe.'

'Oh, I'm not worried,' Mr Scaiffe replied surprisingly. 'It's all an illusion of course, a sudden glimpse of the past. Yes, that's it. Quick, I want to see more before it all vanishes...'

And he followed Ben down the stairs and out on to the Common where the highwayman was now standing gazing up at the man on the horse, as though afraid that he too might vanish.

'I'm not Sir Roger Farthing,' the man was saying, 'I'm Lord Farthing. The title was given to my family by King Charles the Second after his restoration to the throne one hundred and forty years ago. It's very odd, my man, but I seem to know your face. Do you live in these parts?'

'I did once,' replied Ben, 'or at least I thought I did...' He looked round him, frowning, for the Common had changed again. To one side stood a beautiful house built of stone with a gravelled drive that curved round a mown lawn. Beyond the house there were formal gardens and to one side of it an apple orchard, newly planted with small trees. On the far side of the Common there was a row of small cottages bordering the road, which although still rather rough, was in slightly better condition than it had ever been before. The overgrown bushes had gone and in their place was a long neat line of trees, so that now it looked like an avenue.

'Isn't it pretty?' said Meg.

And it was. There were people strolling about and stopping to talk to each other, and a boy was driving a herd of shaggy-coated goats with a stick and whistling between his teeth as he went. A little girl was chasing a kitten, and a man astride an enormous carthorse clumped past slowly, pulling at a piece of his hair as he went.

Lord Farthing returned this gesture of respect by raising his hand in salute and then turned back to Ben who was thinking deeply.

'I did once, I'm sure of it,' Ben said. 'It looks like where I used to live and then again it doesn't. I've had a bad fever, your lordship, perhaps that accounts for it.'

'You look fit enough now,' replied Lord Farthing. 'What is your occupation?'

'M'lord, I used to be a stable-lad and that's what I'd like to be again if I could get the chance. I'm fond of horses.'

'You, sir.' Lord Farthing nodded at Mr Scaiffe who was standing stiff as a ramrod and hardly daring to breathe in case the illusion vanished.

'Would you vouch for this fellow?'

'Yes, go on, say yes,' hissed Edward, '*please.*'

'Yes, your lordship,' Mr Scaiffe said obediently.

'Very well, I'll give you a trial,' Lord Farthing said to Ben. 'I'm in need of a second coachman and I like to employ local men if possible. It has always been a tradition in my family.'

'Thank you, sir,' Ben said, 'I won't let you down, not never I won't. It's like the end of a bad dream for me, coming back here. I must have had the fever worse than what I realized. Thank you, sir. And thank you too,' he added, and much to Mr Scaiffe's embarrassment Ben went down on one knee and kissed the Borough Surveyor's hand.

'That felt extraordinarily real,' Mr Scaiffe murmured. 'Not at all, not at all. Glad to be of service. My lord, might I just continue looking round these houses? I'm an architect by profession and I find them most interesting.'

'Do by all means.' Lord Farthing swung himself down off his horse and handed the bridle to Ben. 'In fact I'd be glad of your advice on one or two points. I'm having them built for some of my outside staff. With London spreading so fast and the price of land going up I thought it a wise move to...' he went on as he moved away.

They went into Number Six, which was the most nearly finished, and Edward and Meg let out simultaneous sighs of relief.

'That was a bit of luck,' Edward said.

'Luck,' said Ben, stroking the horse's silky neck, 'it's more than luck to my way of thinking. I don't understand what's happened nor never will – so I shan't try. All I do know is that I'm home again safe and sound, back where I belong.'

'It's not your own time you know,' Edward said cautiously, 'you've moved on quite a bit since – since...' He stopped uncomfortably.

'Since I was a highwayman you mean,' Ben finished calmly. 'That's all over and done with, that is, and I won't let you down. That's twice you've saved me and I want to repay you, see.'

'Oh, that's all right,' said Edward.

'No it's not,' Ben contradicted him. 'I want to pay my debts and start fair and square all over again. Remember I told you once that I'd done all right for myself? Well, I don't want no part of my old life. I give it all to you.'

'What?' Edward asked, puzzled.

'The stuff as I took off that fat old gent. It wasn't his neither, because I heard him squawking about it being funds for that Parliament lot, see? Well now it's yours. I buried it,' and he laughed gently, 'where I knew they'd never look – under the gibbet oak where they'd already hung one of us highwaymen. I daresay you may have noticed...'

'Yes,' said Edward, shuddering as he recalled the desolate common and the bony thing which had rattled as it hung from the branch of the tree.

'I don't know what you mean,' said Meg, smiling at the little girl who had come up to show Tommy the kitten.

'Never mind,' Edward said with a ghost of a wink at Ben. 'Well if you're sure. I don't quite know what to say.'

It was, in fact, rather a problem for should he or should he not accept Ben's unexpected gift?

'Take it,' said Ben, 'just to please me. This way I can really start all over again, see. It puts me conscience at rest and I reckon you deserve the stuff if anybody does.'

'Then thank you very much,' Edward replied.

'Shake hands,' said Ben.

They did, all three of them including Tommy, which made Ben laugh. And then Lord Farthing and Mr Scaiffe reappeared talking earnestly, and the last Edward and Meg saw of Ben was him leading away his master's horse with an enormous smile on his face and a very springy tread, as though he had indeed thrown away a great burden.

'Most interesting,' Lord Farthing said to Mr Scaiffe, 'and thank you very much for all your advice. I must say you have some most far-thinking ideas on building matters. Damp courses, ventilation, sliding-window fastenings – I hardly know what the words mean.'

'I think we'd better go now,' whispered Edward who was slightly worried that Mr Scaiffe might start to get really far-fetched ideas, such as central heating or constant hot water, in which case Lord Farthing might question his sanity.

'Must we?' said Mr Scaiffe. 'I thought of bringing up the subject of main drainage...'

'Yes,' said Edward firmly. 'Goodbye, Lord Farthing. I think your houses are jolly nice and I hope nobody ever knocks them down.'

'So do I, my boy,' said Lord Farthing, chuckling.

They shook hands all round, and then Edward pulled Meg and Mr Scaiffe round the back of the row, carefully choosing the back garden-to-be of Number One, and wished...

'Do you know,' said Mr Scaiffe, 'I've just had the most extraordinary illusion. I thought I could suddenly see these houses being built. I even gave Lord Farthing—he was the local landlord you know—some advice. I suppose it's because I've had the Row so much on my mind recently.'

'Quite possibly,' Edward agreed.

'And I could have sworn,' Mr Scaiffe went on, 'that I'd just gone into Number Three with Mr Chirk. I must have been overworking. Oh well, I'd better go and have a word with him. I wish I *had* mentioned main drainage though...'

'I'm jolly glad he didn't,' Edward said as Mr Scaiffe, still nodding and muttering to himself, hurried off to be greeted by a very cross and extremely puzzled Mr Chirk. 'It was good about Ben, wasn't it? And the money—fancy us having a highwayman's hoard. Oh!'

'I wish we could have stayed longer,' said Meg, putting Tommy down on the grass. 'I liked it there. Why did you say Oh?'

'Because,' Edward said slowly, 'because the—er—oak tree must have been chopped down years and years ago and so we don't know at all where the money's buried, do we?'

'Oh!' said Meg in her turn. 'Tommy, take that stone out of your mouth this moment, you naughty boy—no we don't. What a frightful swiz!'

13. *Unburied Treasure*

ALTHOUGH he knew he must be suffering from over-work Mr Scaiffe was one of those people who can't stop doing a job until it is absolutely finished, and so a couple of mornings later, with a sheaf of papers in his hand and deep shadows under his eyes, he called an emergency meeting in the front parlour of the Misses Witcham's house.

Everybody had clung to the faint hope that he might be able to save the Row, but after one look at Mr Scaiffe's face they knew that he had not succeeded.

'It boils down to money,' Mr Scaiffe said heavily. 'I've been through and through the figures to try to prune them, but even cutting all the corners we still can't convert under nine thousand pounds.'

'But if you *need* a Home?' the Commander said desperately.

'We can buy a house for less than that,' Mr Scaiffe replied. 'Of course it wouldn't be nearly so pleasant, but...' and he shrugged.

'Isn't there any way of raising the money?' asked Miss Lily.

'I've tried,' Mr Scaiffe smiled bleakly. 'I've tried every way I know, both officially and unofficially, to get a loan. I can't tell you how sorry I am and how responsible I feel for raising your hopes.'

'You've done your best,' the Commander said gruffly, 'we're very grateful for that. At least you listened to us, which is more than I can say for some.'

'Hear, hear,' said Miss Lily. 'Oh I do wish that I could...'

'Couldn't you?' pleaded Miss Rose and then subsided as her sister shot her a warning glance.

'How long have we got?' the Commander asked, bracing himself.

'A week,' Mr Scaiffe replied in a low voice.

'I see,' the Commander said, 'one week in which to abandon ship. Well there it is. No good making a fuss about it. If you'll excuse me...' And he hurried out, for once not looking where he was going and almost bumping into the door. They watched him walk across the Common with his shoulders no longer braced so that he suddenly looked a great deal older.

'I'm sorry,' Mr Scaiffe said again, 'truly sorry. Good morning...'

'Look,' Edward said as soon as they heard the front door shut, 'there's still the highwayman's gold. We've got to find it, somehow. Supposing I went back to that time again?' It was a frightening thought for he remembered only too well what the Common had been like then, not to mention the Gibbet...

'That was then and this is now,' said Miss Lily, making her hair stand up in tufts with her bent fingers. 'So we'd be none the wiser. No matter what kind of marker you left it would have been destroyed long ago. No, our only hope is to work out where the tree actually stood. Rose, that last book from the library—the one with all the pictures in it. Edward clear the table, Meg get some paper and a pencil out of the table drawer. Tommy dear, don't eat the end of that rocker.'

The book smelt musty and the print was very small and there was a great deal of it, and Edward realized for the first time just how hard the two sisters had been working to try to save the Row.

'Now then,' said Miss Lily, 'we'll begin all over again. The moment you see a picture you recognize tell me and we'll try to work out exactly where it is on this map...'

It was maddeningly slow work for it was extremely difficult trying to visualize exactly where places had once been. More books were hastily fetched from the library. Edward and Meg drew map after map, only to scrunch them up and throw them away.

'We'll never do it, we'll never do it,' she said. 'And Mum says I've got to start packing up my things this afternoon.'

Edward had the same job to do himself at Number Six, and it seemed to bring the shadow of the flats even closer as he tied up parcels of books and wrapped the Commander's ornaments in sheets of newspaper.

'Hard at it I see,' said Mr Chirk, paying one of his unexpected and unappreciated visits. 'Soon have you settled in your new home, Commander. Made your arrangements about your dog yet?'

The Commander bared his own teeth in an expression which made him look remarkably like Jellicoe, and then stumped off with surprising speed as he heard the boys from the Common crashing over the wall. He was so furious with Mr Chirk and looked so fierce that the boys, for once, got the fright of their lives and ran for it without being cheeky.

It was when they had only forty-eight hours of freedom left that Edward, who had a terrible headache from so much concentration, shouted:

'GOT IT!'

Tommy tumbled right over on the hearthrug and Meg nearly fell off her chair.

'There,' said Edward not quite steadily. 'If you put all three drawings side by side and then the map here and – Meg give us that pencil – trace it there, see – well, it fits. It all fits together. The pond's gone of course and the road's much wider – wider than we realized, and the avenue wasn't planted till about one hundred and fifty years ago, so the oak was closer in. There!' And he pointed.

'But that's where those other houses used to be,' said Miss Rose. 'The ones they've already pulled down, where you rescued me from that beastly bramble. Nasty things brambles.'

'Imagine having a gibbet in your front garden and

never knowing it,' said Miss Lily. 'Perhaps it was just as well. Oh Edward, are you *really* sure?'

Edward nodded violently and sat down feeling quite exhausted; then another thought occurred to him and he sat bolt upright.

'How are we going to get at the money?' he asked.

'Dig,' said Miss Rose briskly. 'We've got a garden fork and I'm sure your grandfather has a spade, Edward. I'll help. If anybody asks us I shall say I'm looking for plants.'

'When?' asked Meg, almost stuttering with excitement.

'Tonight. As soon as the workmen go home and the rush hour is over. No need to make ourselves too conspicuous. No point in looking for.'

'Trouble,' supplied Edward. 'Right. Seven o'clock.'

Miss Lily snapped all the books shut and reached for another one which had been pushed aside.

'And while you're digging,' she said, 'I shall have to do some more homework.'

Edward told his grandfather that he'd promised to help Miss Rose with some spade work (true enough) and the Commander, staring out of the window with a very sad expression on his face, said:

'I suppose she wants to take some of her favourite plants with her, though where she'll stow them in a flat I don't know. Probably some rule against it anyway. Going to see the vet tomorrow, Edward.'

'Don't,' said Edward. 'Please, just one more day.'

'No good putting off unpleasant things, my boy.'

'I'll take him the day after—if I have to,' said Edward, 'I swear it.'

The Commander sighed heavily and then said with a flicker of his old spirit:

'There's another dratted postman hanging about out there, third time I've seen the feller. What's he think he's up to?'

Edward had more important matters than postmen on his mind, and by five to seven he was moving from foot to foot in the deserted, brambly garden of the derelict house. He was joined very shortly by Meg, who was carrying a trowel, and then the tall figure of Miss Rose appeared hurrying across the common. She had a fork and a lantern which she put down to one side of the bushes.

'About here, I think,' said Edward and rolled up his sleeves and started digging. It was quite a small front garden, but nevertheless it was big enough to make Edward soon very much aware of muscles he had never known he had.

'Stop!' ordered Miss Rose, seeing his scarlet face even in the twilight. 'Me next.'

'But—' said Edward, breathing deeply.

'Not too old to dig. Gardening keeps me,' replied Miss Rose.

'Fit,' added Meg who was doing her bit with the trowel.

The twilight deepened and a thin moon rose above the housetops, and the lights of the traffic on the road moved backwards and forwards. The street lamps came on, their yellow glow taking the colour out of everything, and Jellicoe snarled at a cat which had stopped to watch them with curious green eyes.

They dug and dug and dug, and as the heaps of earth mounted up behind them, their first excitement gave way to a dulling disappointment. Yet not one of them would have given up.

'It *must* be here, it *must*,' grunted Miss Rose.

'Unless somebody else found it first,' said Edward, who had read about Egyptian tomb robbers.

'Don't even suggest such a thing,' snapped Miss Rose.

The cat, getting bored, jumped down from its perch on to some broken brickwork and strolled across the heaps of earth. Jellicoe, old though he might be, was not past giving such impudence a lesson and he sprang across the now very deep trench with a furious bark. Unfortunately he misjudged his leap and fell right in, and the cat twisting her face into something remarkably like a smile strolled on.

'You stupid animal,' said Edward, who had nearly been knocked off his balance by two stone of very solid Jellicoe, 'get out of it.'

But Jellicoe, to restore his own injured dignity, began to dig too, his stiff old paws burrowing away and sending up a shower of dirt.

'Stop it!' ordered Edward, who had been hit in the face by a flying stone. 'Stop it! Ouch!'

The second stone had hit his spectacles fair and square and there was an ominous cracking sound and everything seemed to blurr.

'Now look what you've done,' said Edward not quite steadily. He was very, very tired and getting desperate, and now his spectacles were broken again. It was very close to being the final straw.

'Stop!' snapped Miss Rose in such an odd tone that Edward and Meg both felt a shiver between the shoulder blades. 'Look, oh look...'

And she picked up the lantern and held it close to her open hand, on which lay not a pebble but something round and flat and, even though it was very dirty, faintly gleaming.

'Is it—is it—' said Edward, holding his breath.

'A Charles the First Guinea!' exclaimed Miss Rose. 'Oh Edward, Meg, dear, dear Jellicoe, you clever, clever dog—it is! Quickly, quickly, down in that corner...'

'And now,' said Miss Lily when three-quarters of an hour later the three extremely dirty, extremely tired treasure hunters returned with their pockets, and a garden bucket which Edward had raced home to get, half full of gold which was so heavy that they had to stop every few steps to take a rest. 'And now, *my* work begins. Oh I do hope I'll get it right.'

'Get what right?' asked Edward, who was yawning as though he would never stop.

'To convert it, of course!' said Miss Lily. 'It wouldn't be any use just presenting that nice Mr Scaiffe with a bucket of Charles the First Guineas, dear boy. There'd have to be an inquiry and probably the Customs people would be called in and goodness knows what else, by which time Farthing Row would be reduced to rubble and we should be reduced to the Estate. Now go home, go to sleep and let me get on with it. Five pound and ten pound notes? No, too difficult with those horrid serial numbers. It will have to be silver coinage...dear me, I shall be at it all night...'

Edward's aches and pains woke him up once and for a moment he heard, or thought he heard, that soft, sweet singing which had floated across the suddenly silent night air on that very first evening when he had broken his spectacles. Then he remembered he had broken them again and sighed, and then he remembered Ben's present and he drifted off again with a smile on his face.

Whatever it was that Miss Lily Witcham did, it was certainly successful, for at a few minutes past eleven the following morning a car drew up at the end of the Row with a tremendous squeal of brakes, and even before the door had banged shut, Mr Scaiffe was knocking on the door of Number One and then, because he was too impatient to wait, he raced along the path and banged on the doors of Numbers Five and Six.

'What is it? What is it?' snapped Grandfather. 'Is the house on fire?'

'Better than that!' shouted Mr Scaiffe. 'Come down to Number One and I'll explain...'

'Extraordinary way to carry on,' grumbled the Commander, 'as though we haven't enough to do without—where are your spectacles, boy?'

'Upstairs,' mumbled Edward. 'Oh do come on, Grandfather.' And he seized him by the hand and dragged him out of the house and down the path to Number One, where Meg was already taking Tommy out of his pram.

'The most extraordinary thing,' Mr Scaiffe was saying, 'but this morning I found literally dozens of boxes piled up outside my office and they were full of money. Full. Extraordinary!'

'What sort of money?' asked Edward, who was gripping Meg's hand tightly under the table.

'Oh, it was all in silver...I left my assistants counting it. They were up to five thousand pounds when I left. And with it came this note. Listen.' He pulled a scrap of paper out of his pocket and read unsteadily, 'Dear Sir, I have heard that there is a scheme afoot to turn Numbers Four, Three and Two Farthing Row into a home for elderly people. I think this is an excellent idea, but realize it will take a great deal of money, so please accept this gift of money for the conversion. As a *very* old ex-resident of the Row I would like to see this work carried out. Yours faithfully...and then the signature's a bit blurred, but I think it's H. Benn.'

Edward opened his mouth to say, 'Highwayman Ben', and then shut it again as he caught Miss Lily's bright, if very tired, eye.

The Commander sat as though stunned for some minutes, while the others talked, and then he managed to pull himself together to say.

'Does this mean that the Row could still be saved?'

'It does indeed,' Mr Scaiffe said. 'I've put a stopper on all the demolition plans. Old Chirk was livid...that is, ahem, we still have the problem of finding some common land to pay back, but...'

'But,' said Edward, 'you've already got it!'

Everybody turned to look at him and Edward went rather red, but he carried on gallantly.

'Those houses which you've pulled down on the far side. They were built on what used to be the Common. They were, I know, because...'

Mr Scaiffe stared at him and very slowly the puzzled crease vanished from between his eyes and he began to smile, a smile which grew broader and broader.

'I do believe you're right,' he exclaimed. 'I had the most strange experience the other day when I thought I saw the Common as it used to be, and there were certainly no houses there then. Of course there was a great deal of encroachment in the middle of the last century when the railway line was built, but that's a point for the legal side to work out. Why didn't I think of that before!' And he hit himself quite hard on the forehead. 'Edward, you're a genius!'

'It wasn't me...' said Edward and his hand went up to where his spectacles should have been. 'It was the Common. The Common wanted to keep Farthing Row just as much as we did.'

'It's an odd way of putting things,' said Mr Scaiffe, 'but you may be right at that. Excuse me, I'll have to go to see how the counting's getting on. Isn't it splendid! Splendid!'

'Come with you,' said Grandfather at his gruffest, 'like to thank you and your crew for all you've done. Don't know how to really, except to say welcome aboard. Welcome aboard from all of us.' He cleared his throat. 'Jellicoe, to heel, sir. Don't know what's the matter with the dog this morning, getting old I suppose.

'Well,' said Edward.

'Well,' said Meg.

'Well, well, well,' agreed Miss Rose.

'There's still a lot to be done,' said Miss Lily, 'but I'm tired and I need a little rest. One thing we might suggest to Mr Scaiffe, Meg, is that your mother might like to take on the job of looking after the Home once it's converted. It would mean she wouldn't have to go *out* to work exactly. Congratulations to the pair of you. Oh, and Edward, do you want me to try to mend your spectacles—again?'

Edward thought over all the things which had happened since the last time. There had been exciting things and frightening things, sad things and happy things.

'I'm not sure,' he said.

'Think it over,' replied Miss Lily and hobbled to the door.

'There is just *one* thing, though,' Edward said. 'Now I'm not wearing my specs I can see all your furniture quite clearly, but when I've got them on...'

'I made those pieces,' said Lily with a faint chuckle. 'I rather enjoy it and, of course, it's easy when they are old and traditional. It's the new bits and pieces that are the trouble.'

'Like the washing-machine,' agreed Miss Rose, nodding.

'And the gas-meter,' said Miss Lily.

'The gas-man was *astonished*,' said Miss Rose, starting to laugh, 'he was absolutely *astonished*!'

'I still can't believe the Row has been saved,' said Edward as he and Lily slowly walked up the path pushing the pram between them. A motor bicycle came round the corner of Farthing Lane far too fast and the rumble of the traffic up and down the new wide road was a never-ceasing roar. A jet airliner flew overhead on its way to London Airport and Edward, looking up at it, tripped and nearly fell over a large stone.'

'Whatcha, Old Four Eyes,' shouted a boy who had come hunting for his football. 'Hallo, lost your specs again?'

Edward ignored him and the boy went running off, punting the ball in front of him.

'I suppose it *did* all happen,' he said.

A postman came towards them with a large parcel under one arm, his van ticking over on the corner by the pillar-box.

'Here, boy,' he said. 'This is the fourth time I've been round with this blinking thing and it'll be the last. Do *you* know a Mr Edward Nobson?'

'I'm Edward *Hobson*,' said Edward.

'Farthing Village it says here,' said the postman squinting at the writing.

'Farthing Row, Number Six,' said Edward.

'Must be you then, sign here.'

Edward signed and the man went off whistling. Edward shook the parcel gently and from inside came a faint yet familiar squawking sound.

'I'm not sure – but I think...' replied Edward. 'Oh, it can't be! I believe it is though!'

'What? What? What?' demanded Meg.

But Edward only hurried up the steps to his own front door and let himself in and, by the time Meg had put the brake on the pram and lifted out Tommy and joined Edward in the kitchen, he had the parcel open. Sliding up and down between the packing-cases and the bits of newspaper were three very angry goslings. Meg stared at them with round eyes, but Tommy laughed and struggled to get out of her arms and down on to the lino with these fascinating playthings.

'Remember?' said Edward. 'Aunty Mag? She promised she'd send me Bessie's next egg, only she sent three and they took so long getting here they've hatched out. We've got geese.'

'But you can't have,' said Meg, 'they'd be hundreds of years old.'

'Yes, but Miss Lily told us that Aunty was a witch, so she must have known how to arrange it, I suppose. Gosh, I wonder what Grandfather's going to say! Anyway it proves that it did all happen and what's more Aunty said that geese were jolly good at guarding property. Do you know what?...' added Edward, opening the back door and letting the three goslings out into the garden where they at once began to nibble at the grass in a very contented fashion.

'No, what?' prompted Meg, who was looking inside Tommy's mouth. 'I'll tell you something though. Tommy's tooth is through at last, thank goodness.'

'I bet we never have any more trouble trying to repel boarders,' said Edward, sitting down on the step and leaning his head contentedly against the back door of his home.

And he was quite right. They never did.

Outstanding fiction from the Dragon list.

INVISIBLE MAGIC Elisabeth Beresford 60p ☐

What happens when a modern boy *half*-releases a centuries old spell.

DANGEROUS MAGIC Elisabeth Beresford 60p ☐

Sammy and Eleanor pledge themselves to help the Unicorn get back to its own Place and Time. But where is that? And when?

THE BIG TEST Roy Brown 50p ☐

A fast-moving adventure story set in the streets around London's Oval cricket ground on the last day of the Test.

A NAG CALLED WEDNESDAY Roy Brown 50p ☐

When Liz and Larry 'find' a horse wandering the London streets, they think that keeping it will be easy. A funny and exciting chase story.

ROBIN HOOD Antonia Fraser 40p ☐

The adventures of the fabulous hero in a stirring retelling.

NO PONIES FOR MISS POBJOY

Ursula Moray Williams 50p ☐

The girls of Canterdown were mad on horses. Their new headmistress cared only for cars – and for passing exams. A hilarious school story with a difference.

All these books are available at your local bookshop or newsagent, or can be ordered direct from the publisher. Just tick the titles you want and fill in the form below.

Name...

Address...

....

Write to Dragon Cash Sales, PO Box 11, Falmouth, Cornwall TR10 9EN.
Please enclose remittance to the value of the cover price plus:

UK: 22p for the first book plus 10p per copy for each additional book ordered to a maximum charge of 82p.

BFPO and EIRE: 22p for the first book plus 10p per copy for the next 6 books, thereafter 3p per book.

OVERSEAS: 30p for the first book and 10p for each additional book.

Granada Publishing reserve the right to show new retail prices on covers, which may differ from those previously advertised in the text or elsewhere.